SANDAL [illegible] D

The History and Archaeology of a Medieval Castle

SANDAL CASTLE: The Keep and Barbican after excavation

SANDAL CASTLE, WAKEFIELD

The History and Archaeology of a Medieval Castle

by

Lawrence Butler

Wakefield Historical Publications
1991

First published in 1991 by
Wakefield Historical Publications,
a body comprising Wakefield Historical Society
and the City of Wakefield Metropolitan District Council,
formed in 1977 to publish monographs on topics
of regional historical significance

ISBN 0 901869 31 7

Wakefield Historical Publications
19 Pinder's Grove, Wakefield, West Yorkshire

Printed by H. Charlesworth & Co Ltd, Huddersfield.

List of Contents

List of Illustrations vi
Acknowledgments viii
Introduction 1
Before the Normans came 3
The Norman Conquest: The Warenne Family at Sandal 7
The construction of the stone Castle 21
Sandal under the Dukes of York and the Yorkist Kings 49
Sandal and the Tudors 72
The Civil War 86
The Castle in recent times 104
Postscript: The future of Sandal Castle 114
Chronological Chart 117
Suggestions for further reading 118
Glossary of Technical Terms 119
Index of Persons 121
Index of Places 126

List of Illustrations

Sandal Castle: the Keep and the Barbican after excavation ... *Frontispiece*

1. Sandal Castle and Wakefield by Samuel Buck ... 2
2. Sandal, Lowe Hill and the Calder valley ... 4
3. Map of the Manor of Wakefield ... 5
4. Sandal Castle from the air (1960) ... 8
5. Plan of the earth and timber castle ... 9
6. Section across the motte and bailey ... 10–11
7. The timber hall ... 12
8. The timber hall: plan ... 13
9. The timber hall: cross-sections ... 14
10. The bread oven ... 15
11. Reconstruction of the earth and timber castle in about 1150 ... 16–17
12. Seal of John de Warenne, the eighth earl ... 23
13. Map of the Warenne castles in England and Wales ... 26
14. The inner wall of the stone keep ... 27
15. Reconstruction of the stone castle in about 1250 ... 30–31
16. The Great Hall ... 32
17. Plan of Keep and Bailey buildings ... 34
18. The Barbican: plan and section ... 36–37
19. The Barbican after excavation ... 38
20. Fine quality of dressed stone on the Barbican ... 39
21. The drum towers of the Keep staircase ... 40
22. Typical group of early pottery ... 41
23. Distribution maps of pottery sherds ... 42
24. Graph showing proportions of animal bone ... 46
25. Map of royal castles in Yorkshire (1460–1485) ... 52
26. The falcon sculpture ... 54
27. The heraldic window glass: falcons and talbot ... 55
28. Plan of the stone castle: Richard III's new work ... 56
29. Glass vessels used in alchemy ... 58
30. A gold finger-ring ... 60
31. Ornaments of bronze and a pilgrim flask of lead ... 61
32. Richard III by John Rous ... 63
33. Richard III's 'New Tower' (The Well Tower) ... 64
34. Reconstruction of the castle in about 1560 ... 66–67
35. Building tools: trowels, compasses and spades ... 70
36. The 1562 drawing (looking from south-east) ... 78
37. Typical group of Cistercian ware ... 81
38. Map of the parks and woods around Sandal ... 83
39. A Civil War grave in the courtyard ... 88
40. Reconstruction of the castle during the Civil War siege (1645) ... 90–91
41. The Well Tower, showing impact mark of cannon ball ... 92
42. Plan of the castle at the Civil War period ... 93
43. General plan of castle, showing Civil War earthwork defences ... 95
44. Constructing an artillery bastion: a contemporary drawing ... 96

45. Civil War weapons: muskets, sword, arrow heads and lance 97
46. Civil War weapons: a contemporary painting 98
47. Powder-horn caps and a pottery wine-flask 100
48. Typical group of Civil War pottery 101
49. Distribution of Civil War pottery throughout the castle 102
50. Dr. Walker's excavation plan of 1893 106
51. Excavations in progress within the bailey, 1966 108
52. Section drawing of the Barbican ditch 109
53. Excavations in progress within the Barbican ditch, 1972 110
54. Section drawing of the Barbican garderobe shaft 112
55. Sandal Castle from the air (1988) 115

Illustrations are referred to in heavy type: eg (**45**)

Acknowledgments

All the many people of Wakefield and beyond who assisted with the excavation of Sandal Castle between 1964 and 1973, under the direction of Phil Mayes and, in 1969–71 myself, have been thanked in the detailed report published in 1983. Here it is my pleasure to thank those who helped towards the preparation of this volume by providing drawings and photographs and by allowing their work to be used. Stephen Moorhouse provided his maps (illustrations 3, 38); the distribution maps of pottery sherds (**23**) are the work of Peter Brears; the cross-sections of the timber hall (**14**) are by David Michelmore; Malcolm Stroud provided original reconstruction drawings (11, 15, 34, 40) and altered other drawings where necessary. The copyright of the following illustrations is vested in these institutions and their permission to publish is gratefully acknowledged: cover photograph Air Views (Manchester) Ltd. (C/T30464); no. 2 Wakefield Historical Publications; no. 4 Aerofilms Ltd. (No. A42490); no. 46 Grosvenor Museum, Chester; no. 55 The Royal Commission on the Historical Monuments of England (NMR 4085/38). The reproduction of the drawing of Richard III from the Rous Roll (**32**) is by permission of the British Library (Mss. Add. 48976). The original drawing of Sandal Castle in 1562 is in the custody of the Public Record Office (MPC 97) which also holds, and has supplied the photograph of, the seal of John de Warenne (E 42/244). The photograph of Sandal Castle and Wakefield by Samuel Buck (**1**) is taken from an engraving at Wakefield City Museum. Other photographs, the finds and the site archive are the property of Wakefield MDC and are lodged at Wakefield Museum.

LAWRENCE BUTLER

Introduction

Stand in the centre of Wakefield and, where you have a clear view, look southwards. There on the horizon is an upturned pudding-basin-shaped mound of earth and two jagged tusks of masonry. That is Sandal Castle. For nearly nine centuries its mound has dominated the southern horizon. This book aims to tell the history of the castle, to explain its building and to recall the fascinating exploration of the site by teams of skilled excavators.

The history of the castle starts in about 1110 in the reign of Henry I, and for 200 years concerns a powerful baronial family, the Warennes. It was later held by the Yorkist branch of the royal family. The buildings we see today were started in about 1180 in the reign of Henry II, but construction work continued at least until the reign of the last Yorkist King Richard III. The ruined castle is the result of Civil War destruction by the Parliamentary forces following the siege in 1645. Too much was destroyed to permit the castle to remain habitable as is still the case at Skipton and Bolton Castle. Instead it became an open space visited by artists (**1**) and poets, townsfolk and school children, historians and archaeologists. The latter conducted an excavation each summer for ten years, enabling the castle's history to be understood more fully and permitting the castle ruin to be laid out more informatively. Such a period of exploration could not be undertaken without many helpers. The three main institutions involved in the work were the former Wakefield City Council, Wakefield Historical Society and the University of Leeds. Representatives of these three institutions participated in the work from its origins to its complete publication. The numerous individuals, institutions and firms who helped have all been thanked in the detailed report, published in 1983.

Part of the story provided in that report came from searching historical documents. Some of these belonged to the Crown or to the Duchy of Lancaster, and are now to be found in the Public Record Office in London. Others belonged to the Manor of Wakefield whose administrative headquarters and prison was at Sandal Castle; these are now to be found in Leeds, either in the local Record Office or in the Yorkshire Archaeological Society. There are also the descriptions made by antiquarian visitors to the ruined castle; some of these descriptions are in London at the British Museum, others are kept locally in Wakefield. It is only by piecing together all these strands of evidence, testing their accuracy against each other and assessing the reasons behind their compilation, that a soundly-based unbiased history can be written.

The other part of the story of Sandal Castle, and by far the greater part in the excavation report, came from the painstaking process of archaeological excavation (*Frontispiece*). That process could only take place at Sandal itself; this

1. Sandal Castle and Wakefield by Samuel Buck (drawn in 1722) view looking north: compare illustration 16.

meant uncovering the stonework hidden during centuries of destruction, decay and neglect, and finding those objects from everyday life and from episodes of warfare that showed the clearest evidence of the past. Some of the detective work was conducted in the laboratory, cleaning and piecing together the finds, searching for parallels and determining the date range. The final part of the excavation lay in the transfer of all the objects to Wakefield Museum where they could be shown to the public who had so generously supported the work of uncovering the past.

Before the Normans came

The construction of the great earth mound of the Norman castle and the digging of impressive ditches to protect the castle garrison mark the start of defences on the headland overlooking the Calder valley. However there are two pieces of evidence for man's occupation in this area before the Norman period.

The earlier evidence dates from long before the Roman invasion. A shallow ditch and a pit or working hollow seems to represent a period of occupation in the Middle Stone Age at about 3000 B.C. In and around this pit were flint tools, such as scrapers for cleaning skins or taking flesh off animal bones, gravers for carving flesh and blades, a type of knife. Along with these were found different sizes of cores, lumps of flint from which blades or flakes had been struck. The general impression of this material suggested that the source for most, it not all, of the flint was gathered from east coast beaches from Flamborough Head to Spurn Point. Within the Mesolithic (Middle Stone Age) communities of hunters were to be found on the Pennine uplands, living on deer and bears, and in the broad valleys of Calder, Aire and Wharfe, fishing in the rivers and shallow pools. As well as the finds from Sandal other flint assemblages have been gathered on the south bank of the Calder at Portobello and at Pugney's Beck. Enough has been found to suggest that hunting communities were setting up camps throughout the valleys both on the gravel terraces and on the higher ground commanding the river plain. There has been nothing to suggest a lake dwelling of the type found at Seamer Carr near Scarborough nor is there any evidence for the herding of reindeer on the uplands. However the link between the valley floor and the upland pastures may well have been established at this time and continued to operate for many centuries.

The choice of Sandal as a camp site in the Middle Stone Age was not an isolated instance because some of the other flint material indicates further occupation towards the end of the New Stone Age (Neolithic). This was a time when small forts or enclosures were being constructed at Meltham.

The Anglo-Saxons at Sandal

After this occupation which may represent little more than two summer camps of three months duration separated in time from one another by a thousand years, there is no further evidence (apart from a few scraps of Roman pottery) until the century before the Norman Conquest. Here we are at the threshold of recorded history. The place name Sandal, meaning a sandy nook or angle of land, was given by Saxon settlers. This suitably describes a settlement set on the outcrops of sandstone in the angle between the river Calder and the two streams descending from Chevet and from Walton (**2**). The place name Sandal is one of a number in

2. Sandal, Lowe Hill and the Calder valley, looking north-west
Sandal Castle is in the foreground; the river Calder is in the centre; Lowe Hill is the central summit in the woodland of Thornes Park.

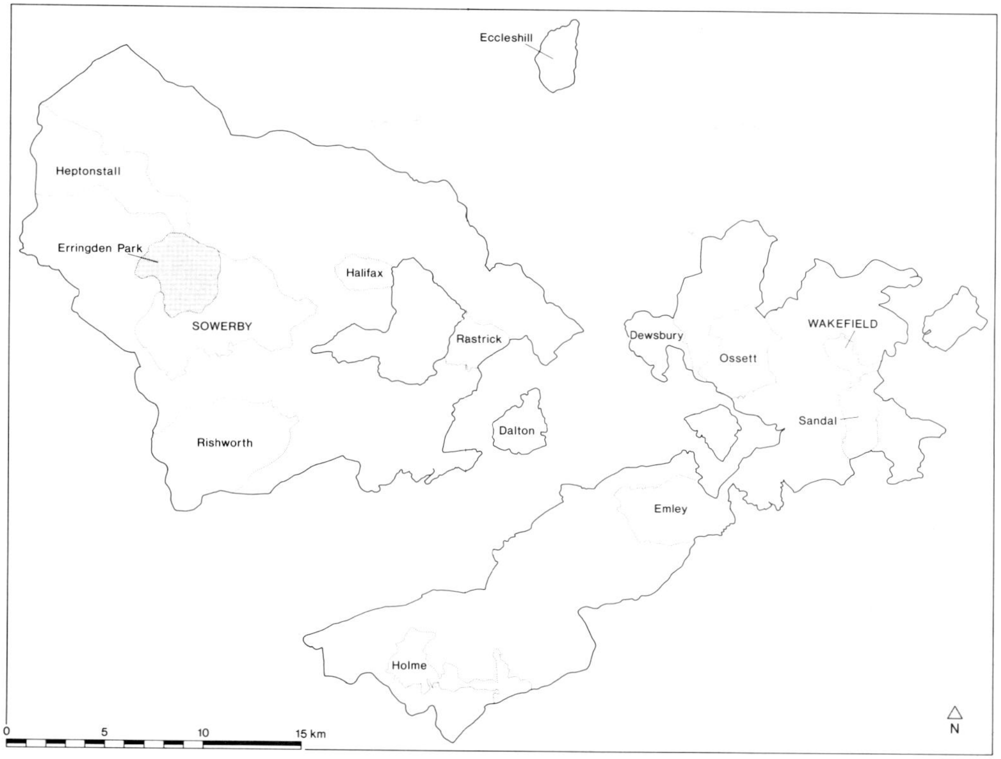

3. Map of the Manor of Wakefield

the Wakefield district indicating Anglo-Saxon occupation. However the usual type of Saxon settlement name linking a person's name with a farm name such as -ton or -ham seldom occurs. The group of names around Sandal tend to use descriptive names such as Crigglestone or Chevet (meaning hills or rocks) or to use racial group names such as Bretton, Cumberworth or Walton, indicating that there was an identifiable number of native British settlers in the countryside south of Wakefield. The name Normanton also shows that Northmen, that is Norsemen or Vikings, were another minority group whose settlement could be distinguished from those held or occupied by the native British from the kingdom of Elmet.

There are two other pointers in this same direction. The first is the way in which the manor of Wakefield was composed in the eleventh century (**3**). Its combination of lowland agricultural villages and upland pastoral hamlets for the herding of cattle, sheep and horses is similar to the fifty townships, part lowland, part upland, described in the Welsh Laws of the tenth century. The name Sowerby-*shire* for the upland part has a parallel in the shires or local units in county Durham where British administrative arrangements are also strong in the early Norman period. The other piece of evidence was revealed when the ground beneath the castle bailey earthworks was excavated. The soil gathered to form the castle had been piled upon earlier ploughed fields. Professor Glanville Jones of Leeds University considered that the distances between each plough ridge corresponded closely to the measurements given in the Welsh Laws. In the absence of any Anglo-Saxon land measurements of comparable precision it is not possible to be certain on this matter but it is an intriguing possibility. The evidence from pollen analysis of nearby soils confirmed that there had been arable cultivation and corn crops grown by the presence of pollen from plants occurring as weeds in cornland.

There are other indicators of a British presence in the area. The church at Sandal is dedicated to St. Helen, a saint popular among the British as the patron of water cults and holy wells. Another nearby place-name Eccleshill (church hill) uses the British name for a church, derived from the Latin *ecclesia*, rather than the Saxon or Germanic "kirk". The great parish of Dewsbury also suggests a pre-Saxon administrative arrangement with lesser churches paying dues to their mother church. It is likely that Wakefield was part of this great parish though by the time of the Domesday Survey the parish of Sandal and the township of Crigglestone were separate.

At the Domesday Survey in 1086 the land forming the manor of Wakefield was in the king's hands. Twenty years earlier at the time of the Conquest it was held by King Edward. Sandal was one of the eight berewicks or "barley farms" in Wakefield manor and was one of only two lowland berewicks. In later centuries it was one of the seven graveships or minor divisions into which Wakefield was split for administrative convenience. The origins of the royal manor of Wakefield may therefore lie in an estate built up in pre-Conquest centuries. In or near Sandal one might expect to find a royal hall or *villa regis*. The antiquity of Sandal and Wakefield as a substantial estate goes back well into Anglo-Saxon times.

The Norman Conquest: The Warenne Family at Sandal

The coming of the Norman invaders brought great changes at the upper levels of society, but for the mass of the peasantry who worked the land their lives were little altered. The followers of William the Conqueror were military adventurers who had crossed the Channel with him in order to increase their lands and widen their power. They were not just Normans but were also men from Brittany and Flanders. Their common bond was their desire for land and their ability as fighters. After the battle of Hastings and the defeat of the northern earls Edwin and Morcar in 1069 there was a new class of landlords like the Lacies in Pontefract and the Romillies in Skipton. Yorkshire was freed from the threat of Scandinavian and Scottish invasions but it was a freedom gained at a high price. Villagers had to pay regular taxes not just the arbitrary Danegeld, and able-bodied men had to labour on their lord's castles and keep the lord's hunting-lodges in good repair.

These castles were usually great mounds of earth to support a timber look-out tower. Banks and ditches surrounded the lord's hall and living quarters, and served to protect his garrison. Usually these castles were self-sufficient residences placed to control major towns or tax-gathering points. Sometimes they were strategically placed to control a river crossing, a ravine or a mountain pass. If they were situated on a rock outcrop the castles would be built of stone as the ditches were quarried and as the rock face was scarped to a steeper profile. This can be clearly seen at Richmond and Scarborough. In both cases the dominating feature is the great tower and not a mound of earth. One can regard the mounds of earth as substitutes for the stone towers.

The earthwork castle

The mounds could take many forms but the commonest was the upturned pudding-basin shape to be seen at Sandal (**4**) and at the other major castles in Britain. Examples in Yorkshire are the great mounds at Tickhill, York and Pickering, three royal castles, and at Pontefract, a large baronial castle. All these mounds are man-made constructed by dumping earth from the surrounding ditches. Occasionally the task would be made easier by choosing a knoll which would provide a start to the mound or by selecting a promontory so that a ditch need not be dug on all sides of the castle. However, generally the work relied on the efforts of the Anglo-Saxons pressed into labour service and forced to pick and shovel, dig with spades and carry earth in wicker baskets until the mound was finished. Then the timber tower and the tall palisade of halved logs could be built. At Sandal very little trace survived of this work because the later stone

4. Sandal Castle from the air (1960)

tower had destroyed nearly everything. Instead we have to rely on the pictorial evidence of the Bayeux Tapestry showing castle building at Hastings and the actual evidence of an excavated timber castle at Abinger in Surrey where the traces of the tower showed by the soft soil filling of the post holes where the timber uprights had stood and where shallower holes marked the base of the ladder giving access to the upper floor and battlements. Around the perimeter of the motte top at Abinger were the holes where the palisade posts had stood in a circle with other posts behind them to buttress the fence and to support a fighting platform and wall walk. Two massive post holes either side of a gap in the fence marked the position of the gate on the top of the mound and steps cut in the clay slope showed where the staircase climbed up the mound side.

Not all castle mounds were as steep or as massive as Sandal. Lesser lords or knights could command fewer resources, or thought it prudent not to outshine their lord. The mounds at Mirfield, North Deighton, Aldborough and Rougemont near Otley were smaller hills, while those still visible at Lowe Hill (**2**) near Wakefield and at Bardsey near Leeds were fairly modest. A castle defence of a different form is to be seen at Kippax, north-east of Wakefield where Castle Hill is an earthen ring, not a pudding-shaped mound but more of a flan shape. Presumably the ring was topped with a palisade fence and within its protection stood a hall and attendant domestic buildings, possibly pre-dating the Norman mound.

Although some Norman castle mounds stand in isolation, the majority are accompanied by a courtyard or bailey. This normally is situated on the flattest ground which in turn is the most vulnerable flank of the mound. The bailey and its ditches provide, therefore, an additional line of defence. The bailey at Sandal was no exception (**5**). The ridge sloped away to north and south, and dropped more steeply to the Calder on the west. To the east the rocky spine dipped only slightly and here the bailey was placed. In this area were all the buildings necessary for a baronial household and for a fighting garrison. It seems likely that the tower on the top of the mound was only intended as a look-out post; it might also have had other functions: it was the stronghold as a point of retreat if the castle was under attack. The tower was the visible sign of lordship — it dominated the sky-line — the presence of the lord was marked by his flag or banner; his legal power might be marked by the heads of criminals impaled on spikes over the gate.

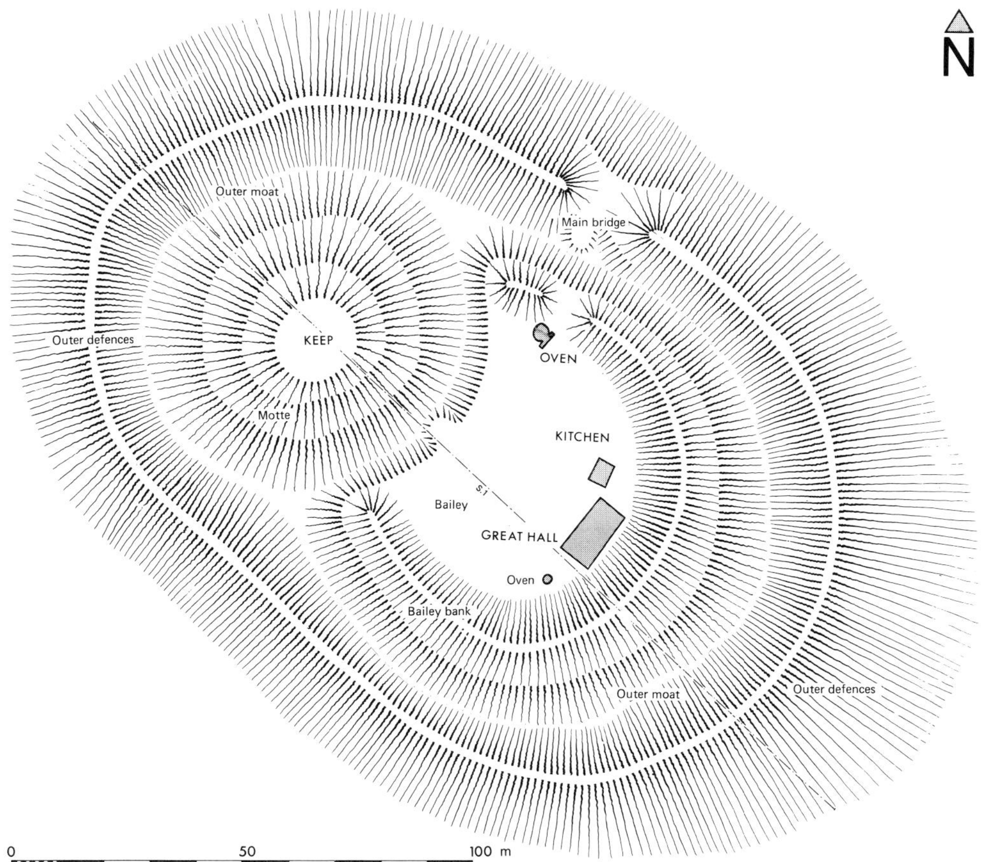

5. Plan of the earth and timber castle
for section S1 see illustration 6.

The peaceful business of living was accommodated in the bailey. Here were the lord's hall, his private rooms and bed-chambers; rooms for his personal servants and those of his wife. There would be a kitchen, larder, buttery and wine-cellar. Probably a bake-house and brew-house provided the household with bread and beer. The well would be a reliable source of drinking water. Other aspects of the household would not be forgotten. On the spiritual side there was a chapel and a house for a priest: he would also provide clerical services of letter writing and document reading, and might also teach the lord's children. On the military side there would be stores for weapons, stabling for horses, and the prefabricated parts of siege catapults. There would be a smithy for both warlike and peaceful purposes, and there would be the store sheds for manorial dues paid in kind whether corn, hay, cheese, hens, honey, hides or wool. Not every function needed a separate building but the excavations at Roger de Montgomery's castle at Hen Domen beside the Severn on the eastern border of Wales have shown how densely packed were the buildings in the bailey area. In the courtyard only slightly smaller than Sandal there were 50 buildings packed together, not necessarily all in use at the same time, but all standing in some kind of repair and using a variety of building techniques.

From Sandal the evidence is far more limited because, unlike Abinger and Hen Domen which were soon abandoned, the Yorkshire castle was occupied by lord and garrison for a further four centuries and many changes to the inner buildings and outer defences took place over such a long period. The archaeologists had to rely on the evidence which had been covered over by the build-up of surface levels and had to identify those fragments of structures not cut into by later works. However the general shape of the castle was unchanged (**4**). The original earthworks were too massive to alter — they represented more than two years work by a labour force of at least a hundred men. They built a mound or motte 33 ft. high (10.25 m.) above the original rocky ground surface and 130 ft. diameter (40 m.) at the base narrowing to 48 ft. diameter (15 m.) at the summit. The earth for this mound came from the surrounding ditch which was at least 23 ft. (7 m.) deep and 71 ft. (22 m.) wide. This gave the mound a combined

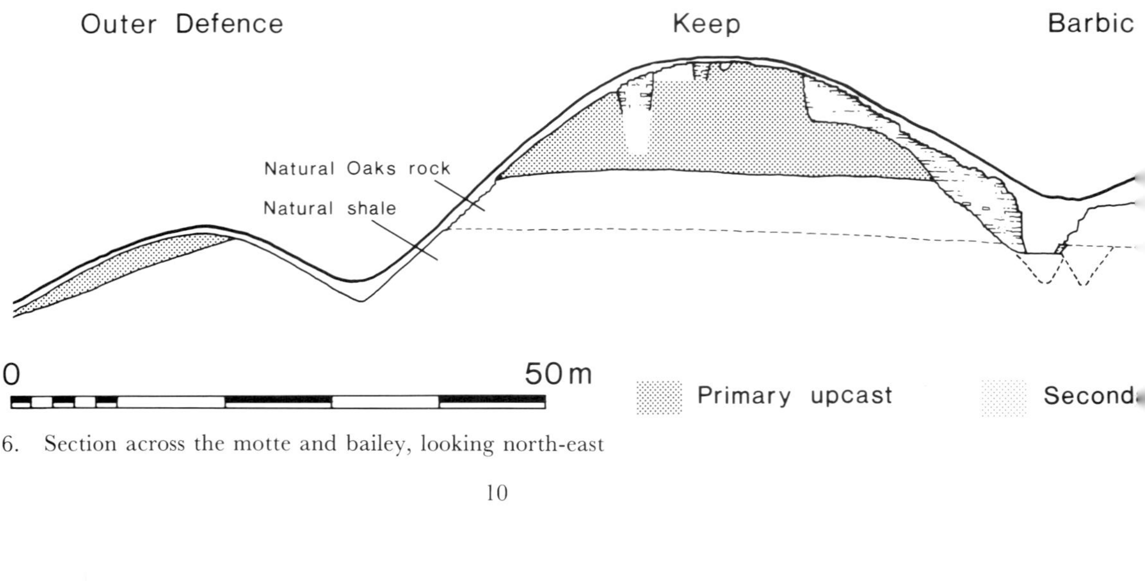

6. Section across the motte and bailey, looking north-east

height of 56 ft. from ditch bottom to motte summit and, when crowned by a tower some 30 ft. high, would present a formidable obstacle to an attacker; from a viewpoint of such an elevation any watchman could command a wide view in all directions over the Calder valley and the village trackways to the south leading to Heath, Walton and Woolley. In the excavation the varied soils and rocky layers that made up the mound were revealed (**6**), just as the Bayeux Tapestry shows in coloured wools the different soil layers forming the motte at Hastings. However at Sandal there was very little trace of the wooden tower and palisade on the top of the mound. Also, it was clear that there was no cellar or basement concealed in the centre of the mound as has been found at Farnham in Surrey, nor was there a well at this first stage of building the mound.

The castle courtyard

The evidence from the bailey at Sandal was also fragmentary because of later alterations and destruction. The crescent-shaped bailey measured 230 ft. (70 m.) wide by 170 ft. (53 m.) This provided ample room for domestic buildings as well as space for stabling, cart-sheds and storage barns. However it is only possible to reconstruct the appearance of four buildings in the twelfth-century bailey (**11**). These are a hall, a kitchen and two ovens.

The hall lay at the centre of the south-east side of the bailey (**7**). It was a timber built structure with five aisled bays either side of a central area containing a hearth set directly on to a compact clay-surfaced floor (**8**). The entrance lay in the centre of the north-west side. It is likely that the hall had an open-trussed roof with hipped ends (**9**). There may have been a chamber and dais at the north-east end, and a service room with a chamber over it at the south-west end. There was clear evidence that the hall replaced an earlier structure of similar character and smaller overall dimensions. Contemporary with the earlier hall was an oven to the south-west, of which a few traces survived, with evidence of two other buildings nearby marked by the depressions caused by sill-beams sunk in the courtyard surface. A second oven (**10**), probably for bread making, was located near the entrance to the bailey on its north side. This oven was of 7 ft. (2.2 m.)

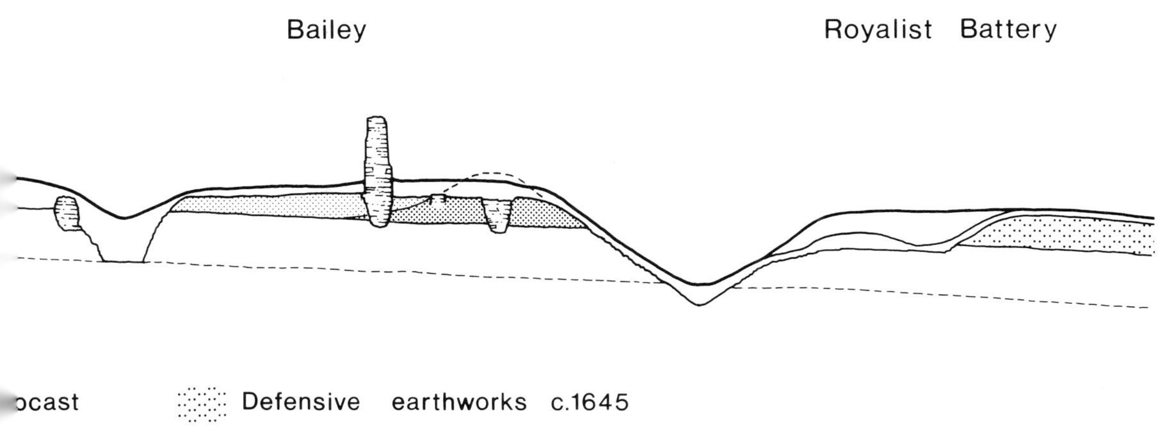

7. The timber hall, looking south-west
On the left are the walls of the Great Chamber (*bottom*), Great Hall (*centre*) and Lodging Chamber (*top*)

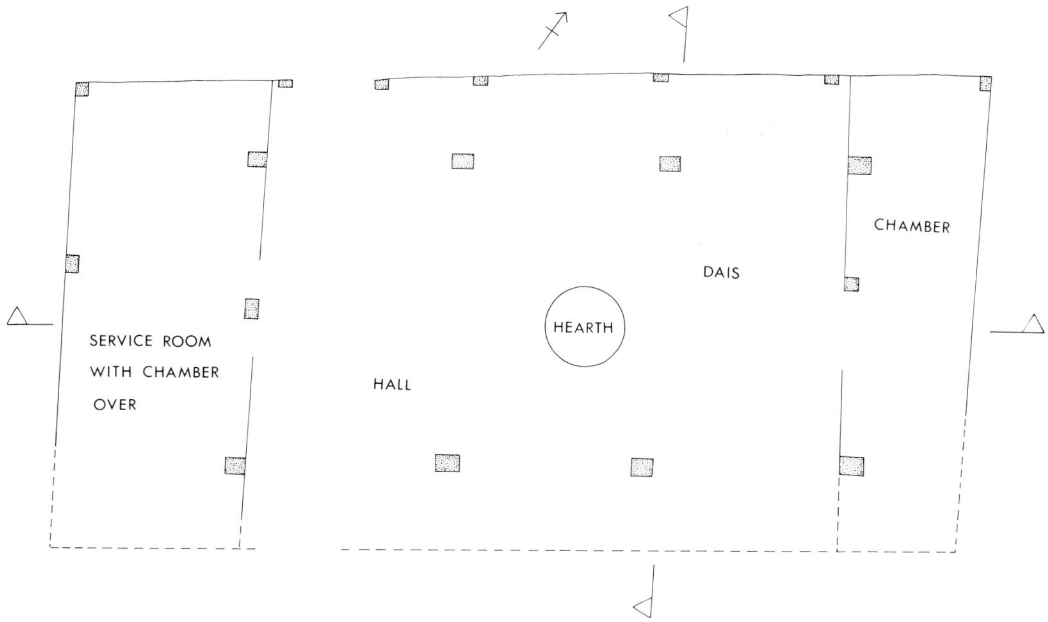

8. The timber hall: plan

diameter, its floor was of sandstone flags; parts of a stone-built dome and facade wall survived to give an indication of its appearance. This oven may have served the entire garrison while the smaller oven (nearly 3 ft. diameter) could have been used exclusively for food preparation connected with the hall.

The kitchen stood to the north of the hall. It was a building of clay and timber with its roof supported on four corner posts. In size it measured approximately 16 ft. by 13 ft. The floor was a compact clay and earth surface heavily marked by ash and charcoal deposits spread from a central hearth area. This charcoal spread did not extend along the western side suggesting that a work bench or seating occupied this side or at least stood in the two western corners of the room. The nature of the central deposit indicated that the charcoal came from a brazier rather than an open hearth. Although there was no clear relationship between the kitchen and the hall, it is almost certain that the kitchen only stood in this position late in the twelfth century or early in the thirteenth century. This would correspond to the later alteration in the south-east posts of the hall. The evidence for this suggestion is the inclusion within the footings of the kitchen west wall of rejected stones from the masonry buildings of the castle. It is possible that an earlier position for the kitchen was to the south-west of the hall, later occupied by the big square kitchen in the thirteenth century. However, the timber-built kitchen showed alterations: it was enlarged by about 4 feet on the north-east side with two new corner posts and additional flooring probably beneath a lean-to roof. From this new area an open drain ran northwards into a sump.

Elsewhere within the bailey area there were traces of occupation such as hearths, patches of white mortar, areas of stone slabs, two pits and isolated post

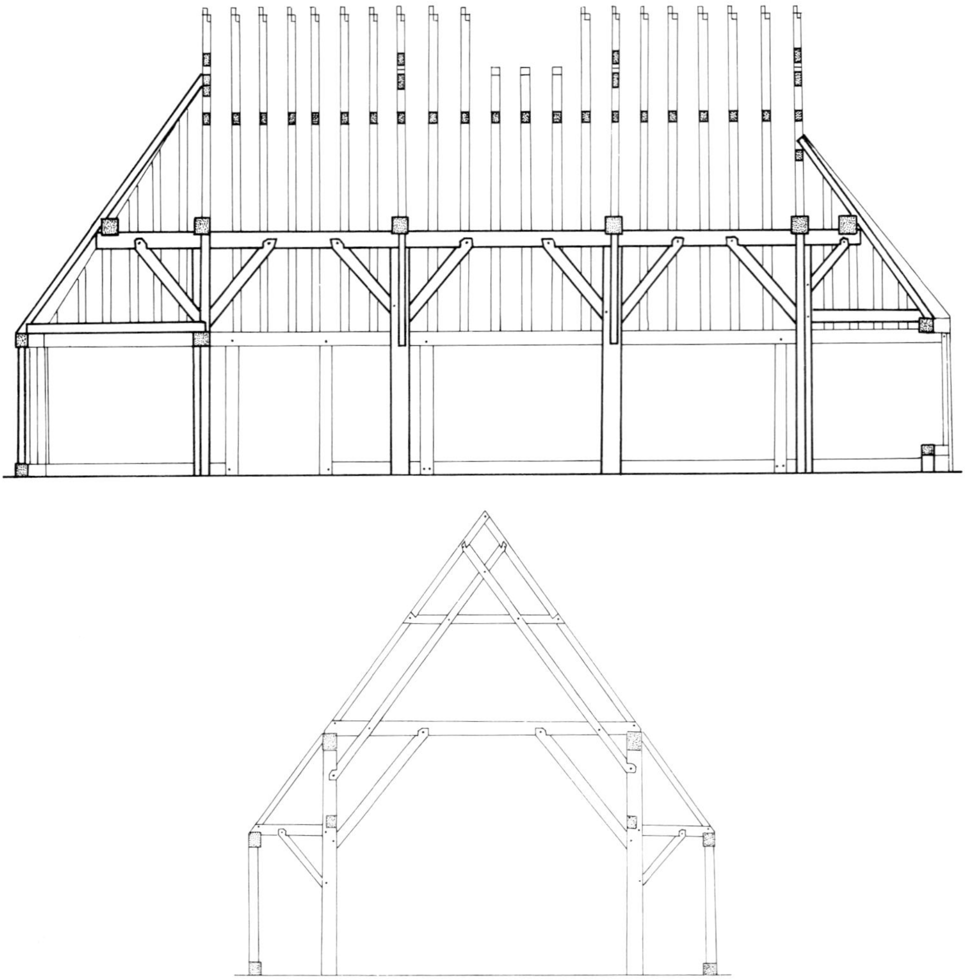

9. The timber hall: cross-sections — east-west above, north-south below.

holes. Such disjointed features are to be expected in a courtyard which would be put to a variety of uses over a century or more. It was a sheltered and defended area available both for domestic and for craft uses. The shelter came from the bailey bank which was thrown up around the perimeter of the crescent-shaped courtyard to a height of 6 ft., with its primary marking-out line composed of stacked turves. It is most probable that a timber stockade stood on top of the bank. However the evidence had been destroyed by the later stone curtain wall which replaced it on the same line.

There was only one place where clear traces of a timber stockade survived. This was on the north-west side of the bailey alongside the ditch separating the bailey from the motte. A gully up to 2 ft. wide and 1½ ft. deep ran across the bailey parallel to the motte ditch, with a gap about 3 ft. wide where a gateway may be assumed opposite the bridge leading to the motte. The positions of massive posts at the south-eastern end of the bridge were found. To the south of

10. The bread oven, looking north-west

this bridge approach was a steep sided pit which may have been a privy or garderobe preceding one later placed close to its position.

The ditch between the bailey and the motte was a formidable obstacle being cut 26 ft. (8 m.) deep into the natural rock and of a similar width at the bailey ground level. A trestle bridge would be needed to span such a gap and to give access to the motte. A similar bridge is shown at Bayeux on the Tapestry kept in that town, and evidence of just such a bridge was found at Hen Domen near Montgomery. The width of the ditch around the bailey was an even more substantial undertaking, measuring 63 ft. (21.8 m.) across and up to 21 ft. (7 m.) deep. Sections of this ditch are water-filled today and in medieval times the only crossing point was by a bridge on its northern side. The defensive character of the outer ditch was further improved by a counterscarp bank which completely encircled the castle but which carried no timber superstructure to obstruct the defenders' field of vision (**11**).

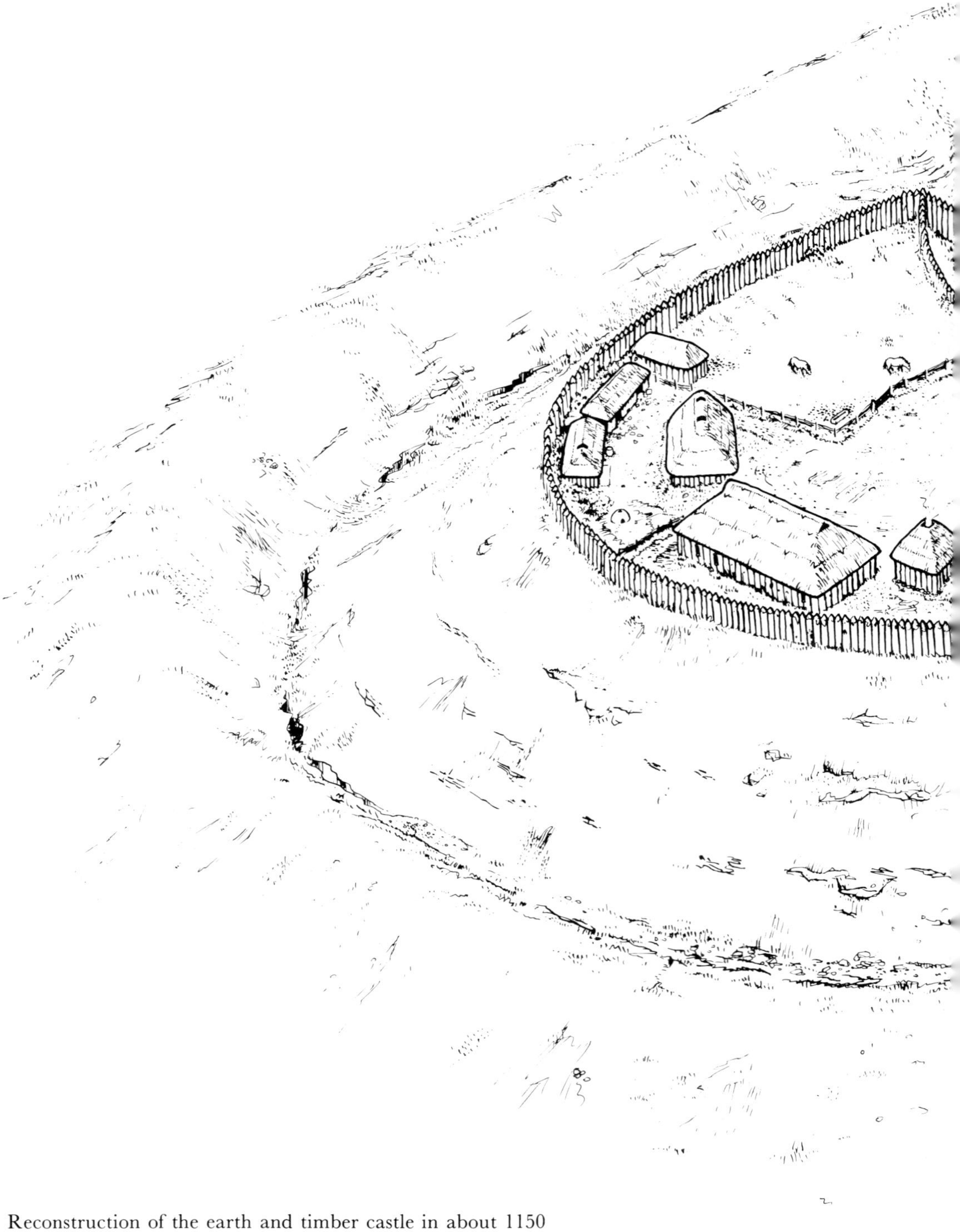

11. Reconstruction of the earth and timber castle in about 1150

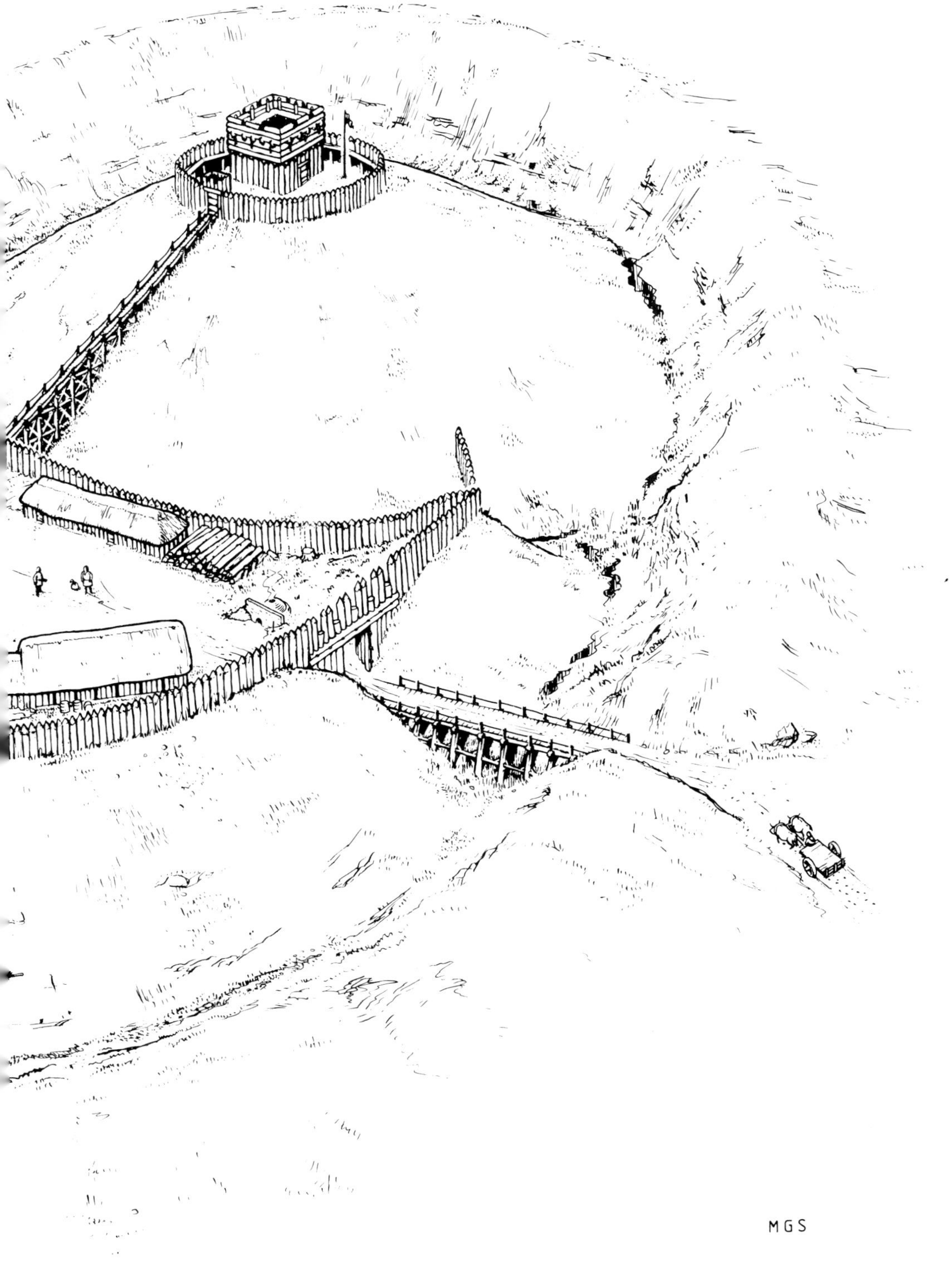
MGS

The description of the castle thus created in the century after the Norman Conquest leads naturally on to three further questions. Who were the castle's builders? What lands did they control? What resources could they command? The answers are principally derived from historical documents and only slightly based on the material evidence from the castle.

The Warenne family

There is no direct evidence about the person who ordered the construction work to begin on the earth and timber castle. The first mention of the castle is in 1240 when it is likely that the stone built castle was nearing completion. The castle could have been built by the king: either William the Conqueror who held the estates in 1086 or by his son William Rufus who died in the New Forest in 1100. The form of motte and bailey castle cannot be closely dated, but one would expect a great lordship such as the Manor of Wakefield to have a defended tax-gathering point as its centre. Another circumstance which might prompt building work to start is when there was a change in ownership of the lands of Wakefield manor: they passed from royal ownership into the hands of William de Warenne, second earl of Surrey, shortly after 1106 and no later than 1121. The new landowner would certainly need a castle to serve as the administrative centre of his lordship, detached as that lordship was from his other lands in England.

The Warenne family was entirely characteristic of the newcomers who rose to power in England under the Norman kings. From an origin in a small land-holding at Varenne on the borders of Normandy and Picardy (**13**), William de Warenne rose in Duke William's favour through his military prowess in his lord's campaigns on the frontiers with Maine and with Britanny. He was equally important in the conquest of England and was suitably rewarded with extensive though widely scattered lands. From his estates in Surrey centred upon Reigate he took the title of count or earl of Surrey, but his main seat of power was at Lewes in Sussex where he built a hill top castle. He also founded the great Cluniac abbey of St. Pancras where he and his wife Gundrada were buried in the chapter house. Her tombstone still exists, now in Southover church near the abbey site, and commemorates her role as patron of the abbey and refers to her noble family, probably linked with the counts of Flanders though it was once believed that she was a daughter of William the Conqueror. She died in childbirth in 1085 and her husband died four years later.

Under their equally vigorous son William, the second earl, the family lands were extended first into north-west Norfolk around the impressive earthworks of Castle Acre and secondly into South Yorkshire around the dominant promontory above the river Don at Conisbrough. In the valley near Castle Acre William founded a second monastic house, placed under the Cluniac rule of its mother house at Lewes. There are extensive remains of this Norfolk priory while its mother abbey has been completely demolished at the Dissolution. To service the castles in Norfolk, Surrey and Sussex the Warennes founded market towns which would also yield a profit to their lords. At Conisbrough the settlement is now more of a village than a town but it did have rights of market and fair; at Sandal the castle was near a village while it was Wakefield that rose to be a town. The extensive manor of Wakefield in western Yorkshire was granted by Henry I to William de Warenne some time in the first two decades of the twelfth century. It has been suggested that the Sandal lands and the manor of Wakefield were bestowed on William as a reward for the substantial part that the earl played in supporting Henry I in his conquest of Normandy, gained from his brother Robert Curthose at the battle of Tinchebrai in 1106. The first indication that William held these Yorkshire lands comes from the fact that churches in the honours of Conisbrough and Wakefield were granted by William to the abbey of St. Pancras at Lewes sometime before 1121.

The first castle at Wakefield

The Warenne family had built castles in each of their major estates in England. That at Lewes has two prominent mottes at either end of a large bailey and is closest in the style of its earthwork to that built at Sandal. It is however possible that the first castle to be built in the newly acquired manor of Wakefield was raised upon Lowe Hill (**2**) in Thornes Park on the north bank of the Calder nearer to Wakefield town but on a weaker defensive position than Sandal offers. This was a simple mound 30 feet (10 m.) high without any bailey now visible. It would have provided a small defensive enclosure while the new lord surveyed his recently acquired territory. Excavation at Lowe Hill in 1953 by Dr. Brian Hope-Taylor sponsored by Wakefield Historical Society did not provide any dating evidence. It could, therefore, have been an eleventh-century royal castle of modest proportions or a twelfth-century castle, initially for the lord but subsequently for a constable when the castle at Sandal south of the Calder was completely in operation.

If it is assumed that the builder of the first Norman castle at Sandal was William the second earl, then the earthwork defence could well have been finished before his death in 1138. He was succeeded by his son, another William, the third earl, who died on crusade in 1148. After this date the estates passed to Isabel de Warenne who became a highly desirable heiress. It was important to the king for him to keep such extensive estates with their strategic potential firmly under royal control. King Stephen therefore gave Isabel's hand in marriage to his younger son William of Blois. When William died in 1159, his father Stephen was no longer alive and Henry II was on the throne of England. Henry immediately married this rich widow to his illegitimate half-brother Hamelin de Plantagenet. Hamelin was a loyal supporter of the king and provided a strong presence in Yorkshire against Scottish raiding parties. He also played an influential part in the family struggles at the end of Henry's reign. Hamelin was a considerable builder and military innovator as his stone-built castles at Conisbrough in Yorkshire and at Mortemer and Bellencombre in Normandy show. The earliest building in stone at Sandal is likely to be Hamelin's work and this will be considered in more detail within the next chapter.

Although the earls of Surrey would have initiated the building work on the castles by choosing the site and determining the proportions, they would have left the day-to-day supervision of the work to their stewards and they would delegate the garrisoning of the castle to a constable of the rank of a knight. The earl and his household would only visit their northern lands on circuit for a short period in each year, perhaps no more than a fortnight every six months, dividing their time between castles in south-eastern England and north Normandy as well as spending time accompanying the king at court and council, fighting with him abroad or representing him on diplomatic missions. The main purpose of the castle was to act as a tax-gathering point and a defensive stronghold for the manor of Wakefield (**3**). This manor stretched southwards from Wakefield some five miles towards Barnsley and extended over ten miles westwards to the head-waters of the Calder in Sowerbyshire. Although divided into two territorial blocks it was a compact territory comprising a wide variety of terrain from fertile arable and river meadows up to bare mountain grazing. Some of the lower ground was poor scrub and heathland, much of the upper land was wild grazing ground for cattle, sheep and horses. Some of the moorland was designated as "forest" and subjected to protective laws where deer and wild boar would be hunted both for sport and for necessary food supplies.

The wide territory contained valuable resources in addition to the crops it grew and the flocks it supported. In most townships there was a ready supply of stone for building and thinly split "thack-stones" for roofing. There was an abundance of wood for timber building construction, while seams of coal as outcrops and deposits of iron were increasingly exploited throughout the medieval period. The swift flow of streams encouraged the building of corn mills in each township and the siting of fulling mills for cloth production in the later middle ages was an added profit to the lord. There were often conflicting uses of the rivers; mills impeded navigation and hindered the steady flow of water needed for fisheries. The marshes and oxbow meanders of the Calder basin provided shelter for wildfowl which could augment the meat and fish diet, though archaeological evidence suggests that medieval fowlers netted any bird that crossed their path rather than catch only selected species. The suitability of the local clays for the manufacture of pottery enabled this particular resource to be exploited in the outwood of Wakefield where the later settlement name Potovens at Wrenthorpe indicates a long established tradition serving the nearby market as well as providing the lord's kitchenwares.

This pottery was the best evidence for the way of life during the first century of the castle's existence. The soil layers associated with the construction period (Phase 7) contained 120 sherds representing a minimum of 27 vessels, jars, cooking pots, pipkins (a type of pottery saucepan) and a three-legged cauldron for heating water over a low fire, together with a jug with a decorated handle. It is not possible to date any of this material on its shape and appearance more closely than to the twelfth century, but it does show the range of household operations that was to be found within the castle. One must use the arguments of historical probability mentioned above to associate the building of the timber and earthwork castle to the early twelfth century and to see it as the work of William de Warenne the second earl of Surrey.

The construction of the stone Castle

The two centuries between the death of William of Blois in 1159 and the death of John the eighth and last earl of Surrey in 1347 mark the period when the timber castle was reconstructed in stone and received the full complement of buildings, most of which remained until the Civil War brought death and destruction. It is ironic that when we know most about the Warenne family and about the building of the castle no direct male descendants of William de Warenne were still alive. Instead the major building projects were conducted by Hamelin de Plantagenet, his son William, the sixth earl, and his grandson John, the seventh earl. William took the family name Warenne from his mother and was known either as Earl Warenne or as the Earl of Surrey.

The earls of Surrey

Hamelin was the illegitimate half-brother of Henry II and remained a loyal supporter of the king to the very end of his reign. He became earl of Surrey in 1164 on his marriage to the countess Isabel, widow of William of Blois. She had previously been sought in marriage by Henry II's brother William, since the king was eager to keep such an extensive and strategically important lordship close to royal control. Hamelin did not become embroiled in the family quarrels which clouded the latter years of the king's reign. Instead he divided his time between the estates he held in England and those in Normandy, particularly the castles he built at Bellencombre and Mortemer. He was equally loyal to Richard I during that king's absence on the Third Crusade and supported him in councils of state. He does not seem to have been so active in John's reign, probably due to advancing old age, but he did attend John's coronation in 1199 and witnessed the king of Scotland's oath of homage at Lincoln in 1200. He died in May 1202 and was buried in the chapter house at Lewes Priory. His wife Isabel died in the following year and was buried beside him.

William the sixth earl succeeded to his father's estates in France and England but in 1204 lost his Norman lands after their conquest by Philip Augustus. To compensate for this loss king John granted him lands at Grantham and Stamford in Lincolnshire, two territories which remain linked to Sandal and Conisbrough for many centuries. Throughout John's reign the earl remained loyal to the king, one of the few nobles who did; he was one of the councillors by whose advice the king issued *Magna Carta*. Only in the summer of 1216, soon after he had been appointed Warden of the Cinque Ports, did the earl desert John and support Louis of France. This was a brief episode and within a year he was giving unquestioned support to Henry III. He served the king on embassies abroad and in negotiations with the prince of Wales Llywelyn ab Iorwerth. He acted as a justiciar and regent in 1230 when the king was abroad. He visited the shrine of St. James at Compostella in northern Spain in February 1223 (see p. 60 below) and founded the priory of Reigate near his principal castle in Surrey. He continued to give generous benefactions to the religious houses founded or patronised by his ancestors: Lewes, Castle Acre and Nostell near Wakefield. His marriage in 1225 to Matilda, daughter and co-heiress of William Marshall earl of Pembroke, linked two prominent families. Their only son John was born in about 1231 and succeeded to the titles and lands on his father's death in 1240.

John was the most warlike of all the Warenne earls and he must be largely responsible for Sandal castle in its finally completed state. In April 1247 he was married to Alice de Lusignan, the king's half-sister. Some English critics thought that this inheritance was too rich a provision for an otherwise modestly endowed lady. She died in 1256, having produced a son William and two daughters. In his early years John travelled widely in France, Spain and Germany. At the start of the baronial troubles in 1258 he supported the king but by 1261 he transferred his allegiance to Simon de Montfort. Two years later he changed sides again giving his support to Henry III and the king's son Edward at the siege of Rochester castle and the battle of Lewes. After a period of exile in France and Flanders he returned to England in 1265, joined in the fighting in various counties and received a pardon in 1268. Two years later he was rebuked by Walter Giffard, archbishop of York, for the severity of his exactions upon his Yorkshire tenants; this may co-incide with building work at Sandal and Conisbrough. When Edward I ascended the throne John swore fealty but he resisted the application in 1278 of the statute *Quo Warranto* (Who holds?) by stating that his lands were gained by his ancestors by the sword and that he (John) would defend them with his sword against all who might desire to seize them. He was equally resolute in his defence of his rights to free warren and free chase throughout his lands. John took a leading role in the campaigns leading to the conquest of Wales, receiving in reward the border lordships of Bromfield and Yale (around Wrexham and Llangollen) and building Holt castle near Chester. He took an equally prominent part in the attempted conquest of Scotland, both at the negotiating table from 1285 and on campaign from 1295, losing the battle of Stirling bridge to William Wallace (1297) but attending the successful actions at Falkirk (1298) and Caerlaverock (1300). He died at his London house in 1304, and was buried in Lewes priory.

He was succeeded by his grandson John, the eighth earl (**12**). The boy's father had been ambushed and killed at a tournament held at Croydon in December 1286. The history of John's adult life was marred by a squabble over his unhappy marriage. It is likely that psychologists would attribute this unstable relationship to losing his father at the age of six months and to losing his mother at the age of seven. Presumably he was brought up in his grandfather's household. In 1306 he entered into full occupation of his lands and was given in marriage the king's grand-daughter Joan of Bar. The marriage was unsuccessful and by 1313 he was living in adultery with Maude de Nerford, a gentleman's daughter from a village near Castle Acre in Norfolk. Since Joan was only ten years old at the time of her

12. Seal of John de Warenne, the eighth earl

marriage, the nineteen-year-old John never consummated the marriage and soon tried to obtain a divorce on a variety of grounds. In politics earl John generally played a moderate role. He quarrelled with Edward II's favourite Piers Gaveston and besieged him in Scarborough castle in May 1312 but he was not a party to the subsequent execution. A more serious quarrel arose with his powerful neighbour Thomas earl of Lancaster in 1317. Thomas had succeeded to the lands of his father-in-law Henry de Lacy on the latter's death in 1311. A squire in John's service carried off Thomas's wife Alice de Lacy from her manor at Canford in Dorset to the earl's castle at Reigate in Surrey. Apparently the lady was a willing captive and furthermore claimed that the squire was her lover. Earl Thomas avenged this insult by capturing Sandal and Conisbrough and occupying their lands in the summer of 1317 and later by capturing the castles and lordships of Bromfield and Yale in June 1318 (he was lord of Denbigh nearby). There is no satisfactory evidence to show whether the castle was damaged in this private war, but the archaeological record is discussed below (p. 43). Both the Yorkshire and the Welsh lands stayed in the possession of Thomas of Lancaster until the rebellious barons were defeated at the battle of Boroughbridge in 1322 and Thomas was executed on a hill just outside his own castle of Pontefract.

For four years after this execution the king held the confiscated lands but regarded them as the property of Thomas's brother Henry of Lancaster. It was not until May 1326 that John de Warenne was able to regain his lands and then the king only granted him the use of them during the earl's lifetime, after which they reverted to the crown. It was a far cry from his grandfather earl John's resistance to *Quo Warranto* in 1278. The grant of Sandal was a reward for supporting Edward II (and indirectly the Despencers) in their opposition to queen Isabella and Roger Mortimer. However with the accession of Edward III earl John again lost his hold on Sandal and the other Yorkshire lands which he only regained in 1334. The earl played a modest role in politics. He campaigned with the king in Scotland in 1336 and was rewarded with the title earl of Strathearn bestowed on him by his relative the Baliol king of Scotland. However his personal relations continued to be clouded by his matrimonial problems. His wife Joan of Bar received an allowance from some manors which she later converted into a cash pension of £120 annually. At the time of the earl's death in June 1347 he was living with Isabel de Holand, described in his will as "ma Compaigne"; she did not inherit any land from the earl, nor did his two illegitimate sons by Maude de Nerford who had renounced the world to serve in the Holy Land as Knights Hospitallers. Instead Sandal and the earl's other Yorkshire lands passed to the king. The title of earl Warenne and earl of Surrey lapsed on his death.

During these two centuries there are more frequent references to Sandal and its castle. The personal histories of the earls are capable of being reconstructed from royal letters, grants and appointments, papal and episcopal correspondence, charters granting lands and gifts to abbeys and the historical narrative provided by monastic chroniclers. In all these sources mention of Sandal is slight and incidental. Only during the episode of private war in 1317 does the castle become a national issue; even then the references are so imprecise that it is unknown whether it was attacked or beseiged, whether it was burnt or damaged, whether it was repaired or left untouched. The private war with the earl of Lancaster did provide one nugget of information because on Thomas's death in 1322 when his lands were forfeited to the king, a royal clerk had to make a detailed list or *Inventory* of all the possessions of the earl within Sandal castle. This list provides a good picture of the military contents of the castle and its food supplies. (see p. 44). Unfortunately there is no information about the individual rooms. The fullest record of actual building work is an accidental survival of a deed attached to a rental of the manor of Hatfield near Doncaster in 1270–1. This mentions the actual payments made to men for their work and for materials while building was in progress on the barbican. However it is first necessary to return to Hamelin who became the fifth earl on his marriage to the de Warenne heiress.

The Warenne Castles

When Hamelin de Plantagenet received the title of earl in 1164 he would have found a castle entirely of earthen banks and timber palisades. On the north bank of the Calder at Lowe Hill was another castle of similar appearance (see p. 19 above). It is uncertain how long either of these earthwork castles were regarded as sufficient to act as the administrative centre for the great Manor of Wakefield. At the earl's other castles (**13**) it is possible to follow the process of conversion from timber to stone. At Lewes in Sussex with its two mottes and a large oval bailey the underlying rock is chalk and the common building material is flint, though freestone was brought by sea from Caen in Normandy. During the early twelfth century a flint-built hall was placed on top of the western motte and then a circular wall was erected to form a shell keep enclosing the summit. Parts of the bailey curtain wall and the simple inturned entrances survive on the southern side closest to the town. A room with an original barrel-vaulted roof stands near the northern curtain wall. The use of masonry laid in herring-bone fashion suggests a twelfth-century date for some or all of the bailey buildings. At Reigate in Surrey only scanty remains survive of the stonework within the ring-motte and bailey, and no firm conclusions can be drawn about the date of the buildings.

At Castle Acre in Norfolk extensive excavation (1972–85) upon the motte has enabled the sequence of events to be reconstructed. Like Lewes the underlying rock was chalk and the common building material was flint; a better quality limestone had to be brought from near Peterborough over thirty miles away along the Fenland river system. However when Hamelin de Plantagenet married Isabel de Warenne the stone buildings at Castle Acre had already passed through three major phases of development. Within massive earthwork banks and ditches of the ring–motte had been built a lightly defended country house with the main accommodation on the first floor. This was an eleventh-century mansion 79 feet square, and it was replaced early in the twelfth century by a keep originally of the same size but with all four external walls doubled in thickness, presumably to support three or more floors of a military tower standing some sixty feet high. This intended keep proved to be too ambitious for the earl's resources or perhaps the threat of civil war was too imminent. Whichever reason is accepted or which combination of reasons are valid, the keep was then built to a plan using half of the intended area. It was completed as a structure 79 feet by 40 feet and probably stood to at least 50 feet high. It was additionally approached through a strongly-constructed gatehouse set in the encircling perimeter wall. All this was accomplished before 1160. No further changes were made to the keep in

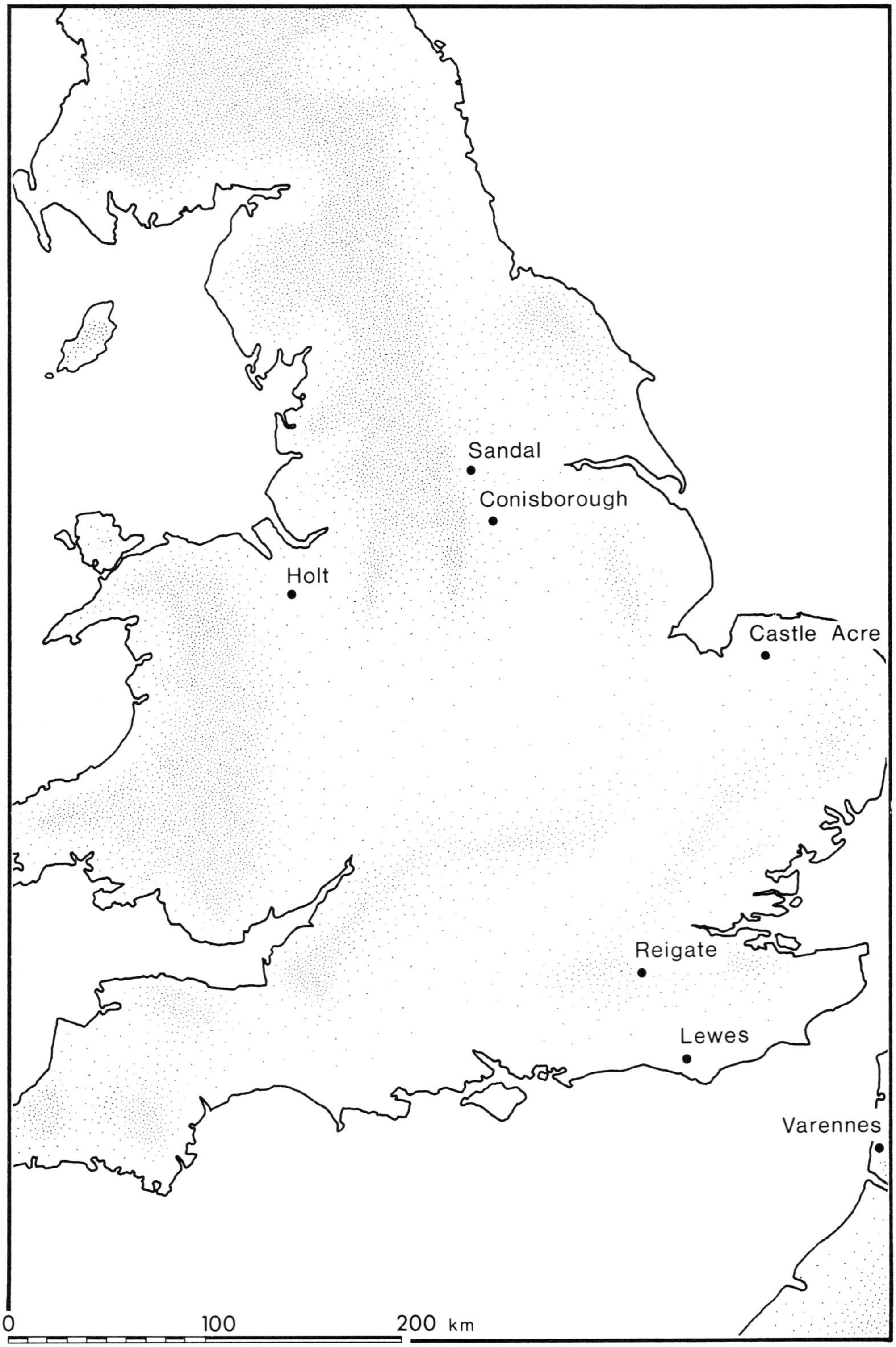

13. Map of the Warenne castles in England and Wales

the late twelfth century, and the main scene of building operations moved to the more spacious bailey or lower ward where the principal domestic quarters appear to have been situated.

By contrast Conisbrough in south Yorkshire shows developments of the highest architectural refinement in the late twelfth century under Hamelin de Plantagenet. The tall cylindrical keep is one of the finest military structures in Britain providing storage, guard room, public and private chambers on four floors with a chapel and smaller rooms in the great buttresses. This keep did not stand alone within the curtain wall but was accompanied by a ground-floor hall and kitchen adjacent to it. A strong gatehouse approached by way of a barbican and protected by flanking towers completed the hill-top's defences. A similar though smaller circular keep was built on the de Warenne lands at Mortemer in northern Normandy.

The new castle at Sandal

When a finely constructed ashlar-faced circular keep inner wall was found on the motte summit at Sandal (**14**), it was tempting to see this "early keep" as the work

14. The inner wall of the stone keep, looking east
On the right is the rear wall of the pair of entrance towers

of Hamelin. However as the excavation progressed it became clear that the inner keep wall was matched by an outer keep wall of similar construction. Therefore the building on the motte had to be associated with the two thirteenth-century earls William the sixth earl (1204–1240) and John the seventh earl (1240–1304). To a large extent the lay-out of the stone-built castle was influenced by the earth-and-timber construction and by the relative dispositions of the buildings within the earthwork defences. A gradual process of refurbishment converted the motte-and-bailey castle into a stone keep and a courtyard castle during the course of the thirteenth century (**15**). Starting with the keep the timber-built square tower and the perimeter palisade fencing were replaced by a large circular keep protected by four semi-circular towers. Two of these towers were placed close together to form a gatehouse and the other two were located on the north and the east of the circuit, the latter containing a rock-cut well over 120 feet deep. All these towers were of four storeys; they contained store-rooms or prisons below and private chambers above. The keep to which they were attached had a series of rooms placed around the outer wall. The "early keep" was part of a cellar on the western side, but on the eastern side the rooms were without a basement. It is not clear whether the entire keep was roofed over as one complete structure three storeys high (as a development from Conisbrough) or whether the inner circle was open to the sky to provide some light to its courtyard and to the inner faces of the encircling rooms.

It is probable that the earlier plan for the keep envisaged a central circle with four evenly-spaced semi-circular towers off it and with a rectangular entrance building at the head of the approach stair. The foundations of this entrance block or "fore-building" were found. However in a change of plan which gave added strength the entrance block with its closely spaced twin towers was built as a single unit. This prevented the inner wall of the keep from being fully circular but added to the defensive capacity of the keep's entrance. Nothing more can be said about the lay-out of the rooms in the main body of the keep but the ground floor would probably have store rooms, guard rooms and servants' quarters, the first floor would have the main hall and clerks' chambers and the second floor would be occupied by the private apartments of the earl, his countess and their immediate family and retainers. The towers would provide well-lit private rooms, each with a lavatory or garderobe discharging down the outer face of the castle walls. Some hint of the decoration within the keep was provided by sculptural details: a simple foliage capital was re-used in later work and three deeply-cut keeled capitals of late thirteenth-century style probably came from an arch or a fireplace. The discovery of window glass with religious designs suggests that a chapel occupied one of the rooms in the north-west tower of the keep.

If the gatehouse block was the second phase in the keep's rebuilding, then the defended approach stair with twin towers at its base was an opulent third phase. (**21**). This staircase was an impressive development, more ambitious than anything provided at Conisbrough and more extensive than that later built at Lewes. When it stood complete it would have given a heightened sense of dignity to the approach to the earl's private residence as well as fulfilling a practical defensive purpose in that the high side walls of the approach stair would trap any attackers and make then vulnerable to the spears, stones and arrows of the defenders within the keep. Even in its ruined state it is possible to gain some impression of the grandeur of this approach staircase (*Frontispiece*).

The changes within the bailey as the timber buildings and defences were converted to a stone castle were equally drastic and impressive (**15**). Before building started some preparations needed to be made to ensure that adequate materials were supplied. Good building stone was probably obtained from quarries on Woolley Edge, two miles to the south, while rubble to fill in the core of the walls came from the local "Oaks Rock" dug from the castle ditches and wells, together with rejected stone from dressing the fine masonry blocks before they were placed in their intended position. During this phase of the construction work the original timber hall was used as a masons' lodge. The evidence for this is threefold: firstly the hall was no longer kept clean of food and pottery debris, but had remains of low status jars on the floor; secondly a lead-smelting hearth was dug into its floor; thirdly a bread oven which served the construction workers (and not the lordly household) was situated just inside the main entrance. Other supporting pieces of evidence were the building of a workshop and roof-tile kiln on the west side of the bailey (under the later bakehouse), the use of a malthouse and a drying kiln (under the later kitchen) and the occurrence of various hearths for lead-working and iron-working elsewhere in the bailey. There were also ashlar rejects found in the earlier kitchen; four of these stones were carved with the same masons' marks as were found on the keep and in the well in the north tower on the keep, showing that the kitchen had served the masons working on building construction.

The supply of bread and beer to the workers is indicated by the bake-oven and the malt-house; the supply of building materials (mainly tiles, lead and iron) is indicated by the hearths and kilns; the presence of carpenters and masons is implied by the nature of the construction work. However the actual arrival of supplies to the building site was most dramatically recorded by the impression in dried mud of the hooves of horse and ox together drawing a cart whose wheel ruts indicated a vehicle with a wheel span of four feet across. This evidence is the equivalent of finding the tyre marks of delivery trucks across wet concrete on a modern construction site.

While the building work was in progress on the motte it is likely that the castle ceased for a time to be a lordly residence and the earl would have used one of his other castles. However steady progress was made in improving the defences and in replacing the bailey buildings (**17**). Although the overall plan had probably been determined by William the sixth earl, the campaign of rebuilding had to be accomplished gradually. The earliest work was the replacement of the gatehouse and timber bridge by a solid stone gatehouse with a straight passage and a corresponding stone-built outer ramp leading to a drawbridge. Simultaneously with this work was the recutting of the ditch at the base of the motte on its western side and the dumping of the upcast rubble onto the nearest part of the bailey to heighten its surface. The approach to the motte and to the keep built upon it was along a tongue of rock, later protected behind stone-built walls. The next stage in the construction work was to provide an outer wall or curtain wall which replaced the timber palisade on top of the bailey bank. The foundations of the curtain wall cut deeply down through the existing bailey bank to reach the original soil layers. In places where the stability of the made-up ground was

15. Reconstruction of the stone castle in about 1250

MGS

unreliable there were built relieving arches or blind arcades; a similar technique was used in the keep exterior wall where the stability of the artificial mound or motte was doubtful, especially on the western side which was most exposed to the prevailing winds and rain.

Within the shelter of the curtain wall two simultaneous developments occurred: the first was the raising of the level of the bailey surface by dumping on it material dug from the motte ditch and the new barbican ditch, the second was the construction of free-standing walls to provide the three major buildings of Privy Chamber, Great Chamber and Great Hall (these names are taken from surveys made in the Tudor period). In each of these three rooms only the ground floor cellar survives in any state of completeness. The main living quarters were at first floor level and only part of the inner side of the Great Hall still stands in ruins (**16**). Each room had a flagged floor, windows facing onto the courtyard and a solid wall to the exterior of the castle. In the two larger rooms, the Great Chamber and the Great Hall, their stone floors were supported on pillars: a square foundation for the pillar below the Chamber and two circular pillar bases below the Hall. It is likely that the ground-floor cellars were stone vaulted; this is suggested by the ragged nature of the inner face of the Hall wall where the stone vaulting has been torn away. These cellars were principally store-rooms. The space beneath the Great Hall has no further internal features surviving. The cellar under the Great Chamber had a fireplace in the south-west corner of the room and two garderobe shafts, one in the south-east corner of the room and

16. The Great Hall (*left*) and the Lodging Chamber gable (*right*), looking east Compare with illustration 1.

the other in the north-east corner of the room which it shared with the Privy or Private Chamber. Apart from this shared garderobe shaft the only other feature within the ground floor of this Private Chamber was a small hearth, its stone set against the south wall; the room above was too small to need its floor supporting on a column. Beyond the Private Chamber to its north was the bailey well, a circular stone-lined shaft, 7 feet in diameter and at least 40 feet deep. It is not clear whether it was planned that a further building should have been added here to extend the range northwards: only a stub wall survived which may be the start of such an extension but might be no more than a buttress. The area between the Private Chamber and the Gatehouse just within the curtain wall was later occupied by work-sheds and a small barn.

It is probable that the main changes of direction in the outer wall were protected by two or more turrets, shown as square in plan on the 1562 drawing (**36**). West of the Great Hall was an ambitious Presence Chamber (much later used as a lodging and then as a buttery). It was approached from the ground level in the courtyard by climbing a stone staircase leading to an upper porch supported on an octagonal column. Beyond the porch was a semi-circular oriel gallery, generously provided with windows and supported on a graceful circular column. From this oriel gallery the visitor entered the presence chamber and so passed through to the Great Hall. The foot of the stair and the bases of the two columns are still visible in the exterior angle between the Great Hall and the presence chamber. The surviving ground-floor room has a later cobbled floor (perhaps replacing a flagged floor), one window looking onto the courtyard and a centrally-placed pillar to support a vaulted roof. At a later uncertain period a second circular column was inserted, perhaps to support a weak area in the vaulting. The north-west angle of this room was embellished by a solid circular turret with a fine external ashlar surface and a chamfered base. There may have been a similar turret at the south-west angle to protect a sharp change in direction to the curtain wall. No trace of this postulated turret now remains. At first-floor level the existing turret probably contained a spiral stair leading to the defensive wall walk at roof level. The decorative finial of this turret was found in 1964 lying amid the destruction rubble nearby. It was in the form of a fleur-de-lys. In the west wall this room was lit by a single-light window which still survives in a ruined and altered state.

All the bailey buildings so far described provided living accommodation for the lord and his household when they visited Sandal for public occasions (**17**). At other times they would be used by the constable and his family who would be permanently resident at the castle. The group of three buildings placed alongside the western part of the courtyard were service rooms to supply food and drink to the household. All three were late in the sequence of replacing the timber buildings by stone structures; mention has already been made of the tile kiln, malt-house and lead-working hearth beneath them in this area (p. 29 above). The central room in this group of three was a kitchen roughly 32 feet square. It contained a roasting hearth, beside which the position of two posts supporting a spit could be seen at either end; two other hearths and an internal drain flowing into the barbican ditch were also found. The 1562 drawing (**36**) shows this building as a tall structure with a stone tiled roof and with a central chimney or timber louvre through with cooking smells and smoke could escape. It would

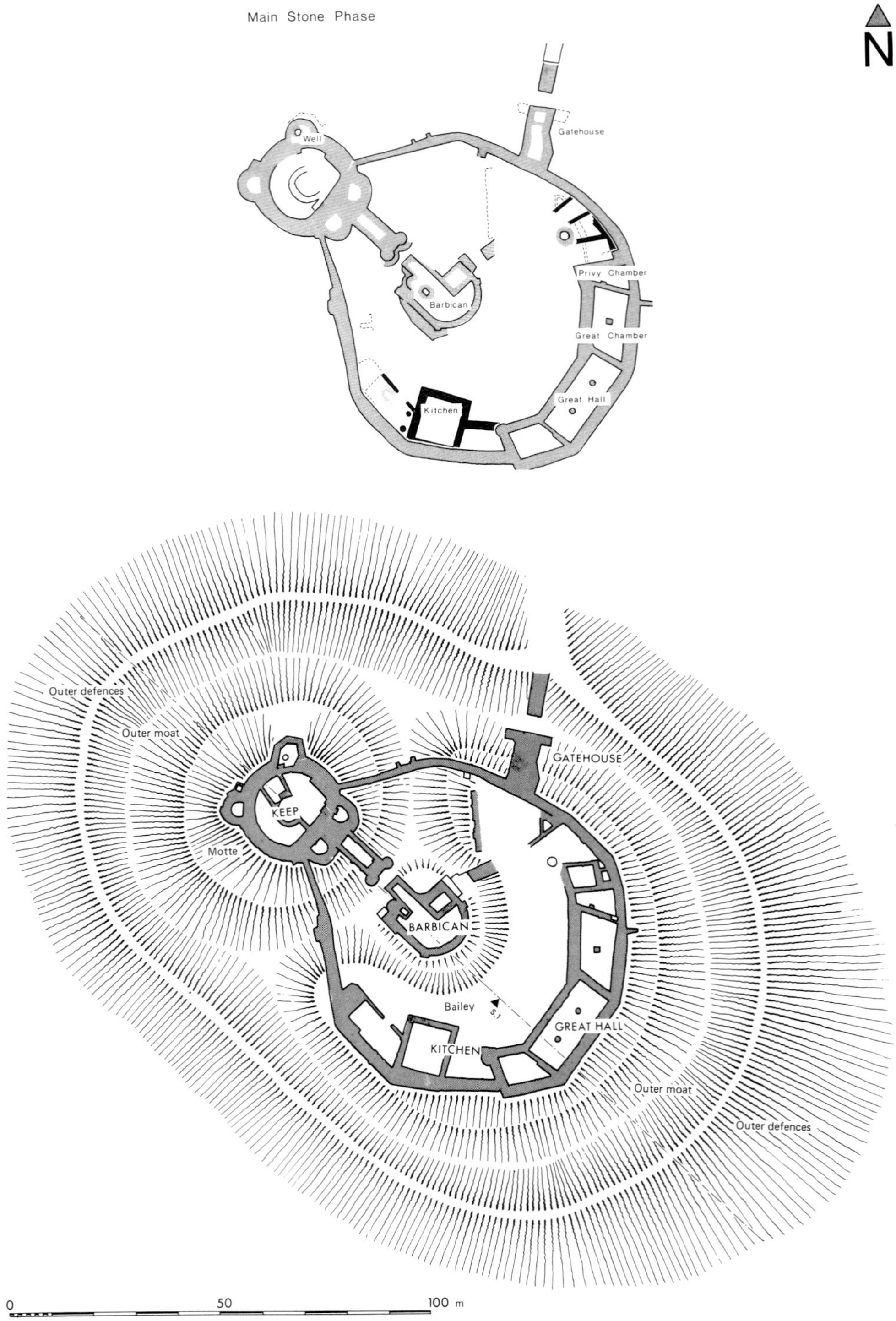

17. Plan of Keep and Bailey buildings
(*top*) thirteenth-century construction
(*below*) buildings in relation to earthworks for section S1 see illustration 6

have been similar to the monastic kitchens still visible at Fountains and Jervaulx, though not as well planned as those. There were presumably small windows at a high level. Adjoining the kitchen on either side were single storey buildings, a "larder" fitted in rather awkwardly to the east next to the Presence Chamber and a lightly built bakehouse to the north-west. The "larder" had two small hearths as part of its original fitting, while the bakehouse had a central hearth and two small circular ovens.

Throughout the bailey area there was undertaken the gradual infilling to bring the interiors of the main buildings up to the intended floor level. The material came principally from three areas: the levelling of the bailey bank outside the curtain wall, the deepening of the outer ditch beyond the new curtain wall and the digging out of the barbican ditch as this new feature was constructed. The courtyard between the main domestic range and the barbican ditch was also levelled up with material from these three areas though most of it presumably came from the barbican ditch. This process trapped all the evidence for the construction work on the keep while workmen were utilising the derelict buildings of the timber castle (see **6**: secondary upcast).

The third element in the new stone castle was an unusual feature — a barbican tower outside the main defensive keep but inside the defended courtyard (**18**). It is the only part of the structure that can be dated. In the financial accounts of the local officials (or "graves") for the year 1270–71 there is mention of the supply of timber for building and scaffolding at the barbican and the related payment of the carpenters, the supply of stone, gravel and lime for the same work and the associated wages of the masons, the supply of iron and the wages of the carters. The provision of "targes" for the tops of walls suggests that these were hinged wooden flaps which fitted between the battlements to protect the archers of the defenders. This provision indicates that the work was nearing completion. The evidence of 1270–71 is supported by a thermo-luminescent date from pottery found on the original bailey surface beneath the barbican tower which gave a date of 1265 ± 17 years, based on trapped electrical energy. As a design element the tower is at the forefront of military planning comparable to the work of Philip IV of France at his palace of the Louvre in Paris and to the improvements made by Edward I at the Tower of London in 1275–76. If the D-shaped barbican tower was an original feature of the castle's remodelling, then this suggests advanced military thinking by John the seventh earl, who played a leading role in the campaigns during the reigns of Henry III and Edward I.

The Barbican Tower (**19**) formed a stepping stone between the courtyard and the keep. Attackers had to cross a draw-bridge to reach the barbican, then pass through its first gate protected by a portcullis, turn through a right-angled passage, fight their way past at least one other gate and its portcullis within the tower and then cross a second drawbridge before reaching the drum towers at the foot of the stone staircase up the steep slope of the motte in order to reach the keep. The accommodation provided within the tower indicates that it was intended to be a lodging unit capable of being held independently from the courtyard: the guard chamber at passage level had its own latrine and stair to the sally port. The rooms above were probably reached by a spiral stair in the circular north-west tower. The friable rock faces around the foot of the tower were covered by a protective masonry shield using as many as twelve courses of

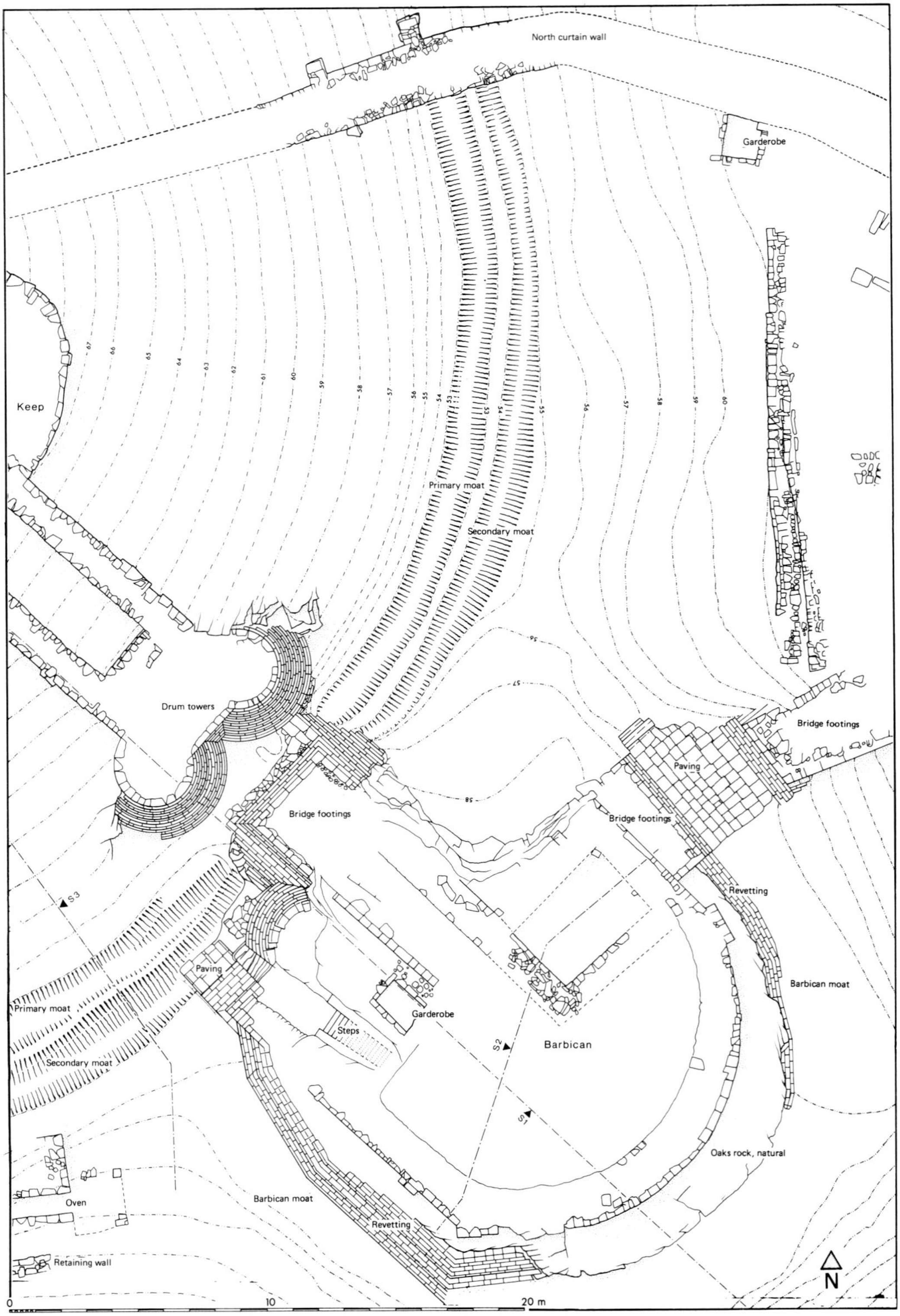

18. The Barbican: plan, and section S2 looking south

finely dressed chamfered stone (**20**). The base of the ditch beneath the drawbridge was paved with heavy, well-laid gritstone slabs to prevent tunnelling or undermining. The ditch surrounding the barbican must have presented a substantial obstacle to attackers when it was first cut, particularly since the heightening by five feet of the interior floor of the barbican and of the surface of the encircling courtyard would give the ditch added depth to an entire total of 30 feet deep. However the archaeological material makes is clear that the ditch was not kept clean and defensible for very long, but it soon became the main dumping ground for any rubbish discarded within the castle. The rubbish was mainly broken pottery and unwanted animal bone. The ditch remained in use as a rubbish dump for the next three centuries.

The main Gatehouse at the entrance to the castle bailey had been improved at the start of the period of rebuilding in stone and it was improved further towards the end of the thirteenth century. The straight approach was altered to give an angled turn and a sloping passage which prevented attackers with battering rams getting a direct run at the inner gate, always assuming that they had crossed the drawbridge, broken the outer gates and raised the iron-shod portcullis. The improvement of the gatehouse was probably simultaneous with the completion of the recut ditch between the keep and the courtyard and also with the provision of flanking curtain walls to link these two areas. These flanking walls which stood about twenty feet high would have carried a defensive wall walk from the curtain wall around the bailey up the sides of the motte to join the keep (*Frontispiece*). However although the curtain walls reached the keep the

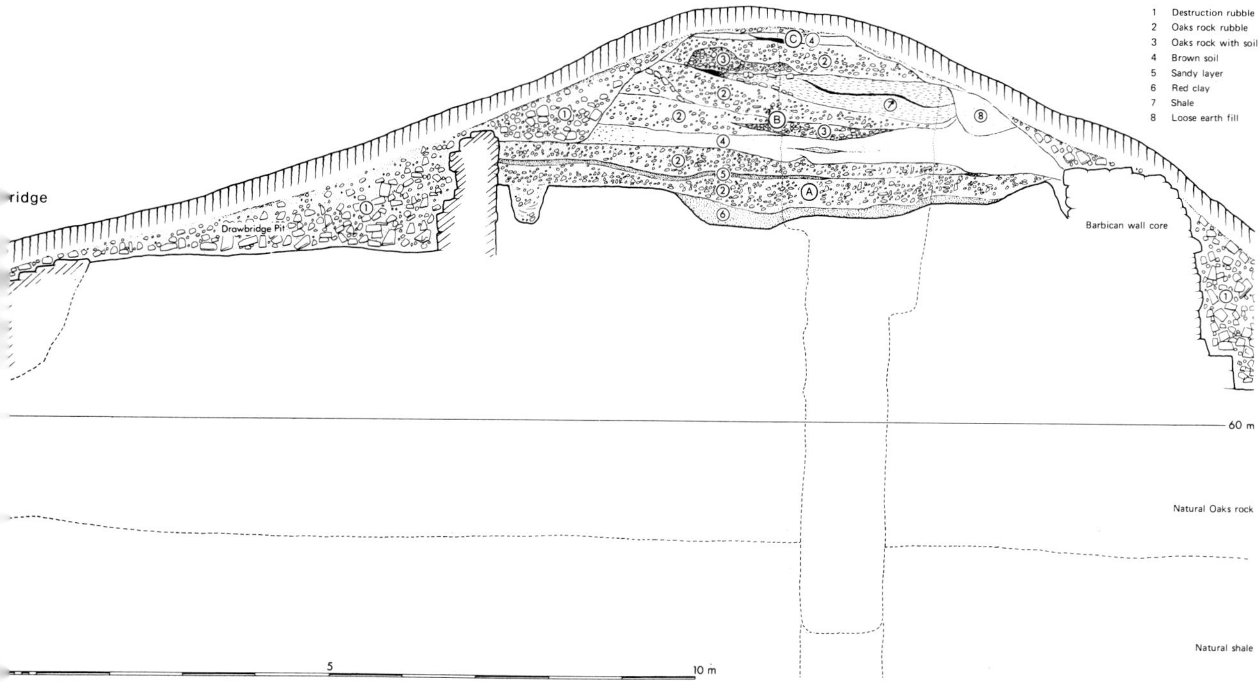

19. The Barbican after excavation, looking east

actual wall walks did not. Instead there is a gradual narrowing in width which indicates that the wall walk ended before the keep was reached. This is directly parallel to the late thirteenth-century town walls at Conway and Caernarvon which narrow in similar fashion as they approach these two magnificent Edwardian castles. Lower down the motte slope where the high flanking walls cross the motte ditch, the walls are strengthened on the west flank and buttressed on the north flank, the latter two buttresses perhaps being carried upwards to form a turret to control the moat junction.

With the improvement to the gatehouse and the completion of the defensive circuit of curtain walls, the stone building of the castle was completed. Although it is impossible to give a precise date for any part of this building programme (apart from the barbican work nearing completion in 1270–71), there are a number of clues contained in the archaeological and architectural evidence

20. Fine quality of dressed stone on the Barbican, showing masons' marks

which show the sequence of the work and serve to indicate which parts are contemporary with one another. The archaeological evidence is provided by coins and pottery; the architectural evidence is displayed in the masons' marks, the tooling of the stones and the styles of carved details. This combination of evidence will be examined for the three main phases of the building programme.

The dating evidence

The first phase (numbered 5a i in the detailed excavation report) is the earliest construction work on the keep and the contemporary occupation of the timber hall as the masons' lodge. The coin evidence is a single penny of John, relatively unworn and found in the construction trench of the bridge leading to the barbican from the courtyard. Although the coin was minted between 1205 and 1208 and its condition suggested that its loss was soon after this date, the coin must on all the other evidence have been brought to this part of the castle some fifty or sixty years later. One must conclude therefore that the coin had seeped into the foundation filling from redeposited soil. However the pottery of this phase had quite clearly been broken while the buildings were being built or used. Unfortunately none of the pottery is capable of close dating (unlike coins), but a general thirteenth-century date is likely. What the pottery does show is the variety of vessel types in common use and the range of market sources from which they were bought. The 2711 sherds represent a minimum of 204 different vessels and 2276 of these sherds were found in the timber hall after it had become a masons' lodge. In this phase the commonest vessel forms are jars and handled ladles (looking rather like sauce boats) with lesser quantities of spouted jugs and a

21. The drum towers at the base of the Keep staircase, looking west to the sally-port doorway

few bowls (**22**). Some of the brown- and green-glazed jugs were attractively decorated with vertical lines of applied pellets, combed decoration or raised notched strips; one had a well-moulded face mask with miniature arms and a crimped beard. Most of the wares were of local western Yorkshire manufacture in gritty or shelly fabric with the finer jugs coming from the Hallgate kiln in Doncaster or an imitator close to Conisbrough castle. The only distant wares were jars from Staxton near Scarborough, perhaps brought with sea fish supplies or coming from some person visiting the royal castle there, and vessels from Grimston in west Norfolk, probably travelling in the earl's baggage train from Castle Acre, another important estate centre. Occasionally parts of distinctive vessels can be found which show that building work was proceeding simultane-

22. Typical group of early pottery

ously on the inner wall of the keep and on recutting the motte ditch (**23a**). There were 54 sherds of a jug in a thick white fabric with a watery pale green glaze on the keep and 19 sherds of the same jug found in the motte ditch.

The other main type of evidence is architectural. Out of a total of 37 masons' marks, 18 different ones occur both on the keep and on the barbican, or on the keep well and on the bailey well, or on the keep, barbican steps and the drum towers of the keep approach stair. Not only does the same individual mason's mark occur, but the same family of marks or the same combination of marks is found carved on the dressed stone. All this evidence suggests that the same group of masons worked upon the project: in some cases they were carving stone for different parts of the castle at the same time, such as on the drum towers at the base of the staircase and the adjacent barbican, but on other occasions they tackled one area until that part was finished, as on the keep, and then moved to another, such as the bailey well. The best parallels for these families of marks are to be seen in the mid and late thirteenth century. The same dating sequence is given by the character of the tool marks on the stones of the keep and barbican: strong diagonal chisel tooling is used on the earlier work; fine dressed ashlar with a smooth surface is present on all parts of the barbican and the drum tower revetment (**21**) together with parts of the main gatehouse and the west curtain wall. The style of the carved details with keeled capitals, pointed arched window heads and simple Y-shaped tracery all points to a date in the second quarter of the thirteenth century for this phase. This confirms that the earliest work on the keep was started not under Hamelin de Plantagenet but under his son William

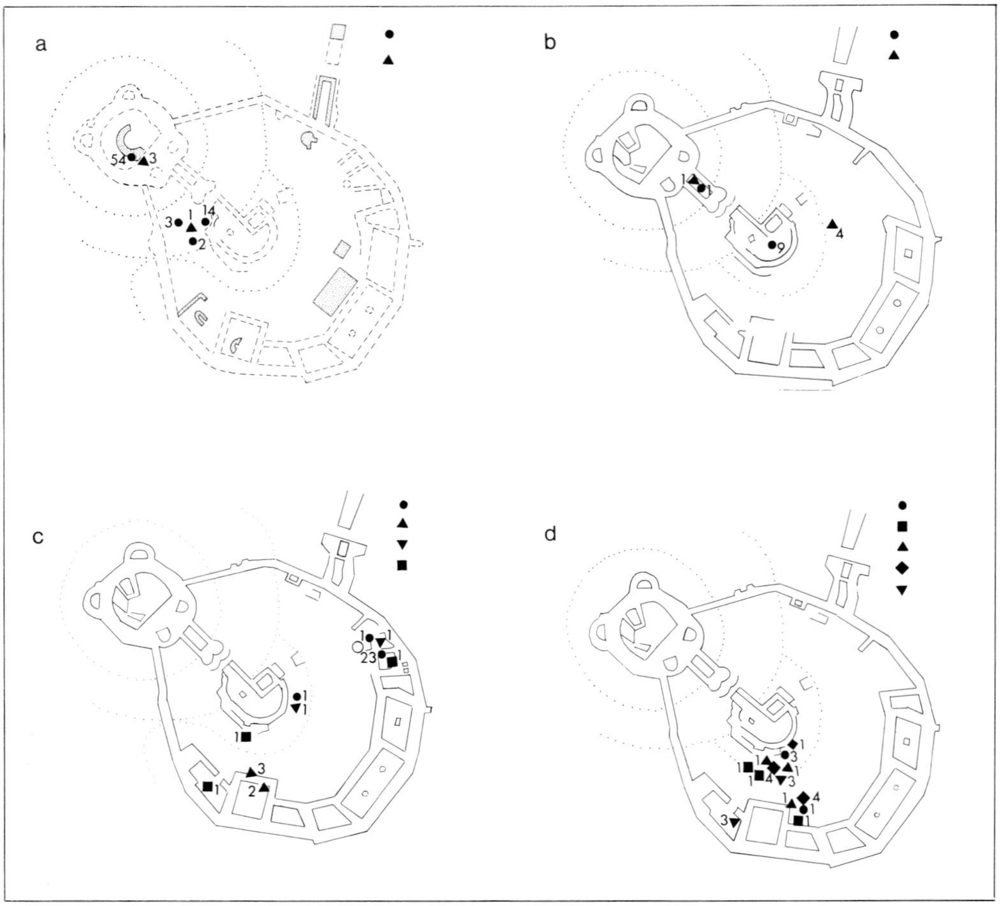

23. Distribution maps of pottery sherds showing where sherds of the same vessel occur in different parts of the castle. Each symbol indicates a distinctive vessel at each phase.
a: occupation of early stone keep
b: construction of barbican and motte staircase
c: occupation of major stone castle
d: vessels linked to industrial activities in courtyard

the sixth earl (died 1240). A royal judicial enquiry made at William's death is the first documentary evidence of the castle's existence, although the earl had appointed a castle constable as early as 1206–18.

The second phase (numbered 5a ii in the detailed excavation report) marks the completion of the building phase on the barbican, staircase drum towers, courtyard buildings and curtain walls. The bailey surface associated with the first construction phase was covered over with loose rock, shale and soil dug from the ditches. A similar range of archaeological and architectural evidence needs to be examined. No coins were found in the layers of this phase, but pottery was reasonably abundant with 1032 sherds representing at least 178 different vessels. Many of the pots were of the forms already encountered, such as jars, jugs and ladles, and were of the fabrics already mentioned, namely gritty wares, shelly wares and Hallgate kiln products. The styles of decoration on the jugs were similar though combed wavy lines running in horizontal bands around the jugs' shoulders become more common and stabbed decoration on the handles is more frequent. The only new vessel form is the pottery curfew, used to prevent the embers on the hearth from throwing out sparks during the night hours and setting light to the rushes strewn over the stone flagged floors. There is now more variety in fabrics with a range of fine red and white wares, most of them from kilns in the vale of York which supplied that city as well as Beverley and the refounded Kingston-upon-Hull. Again it is possible to see building work going on simultaneously with sherds of related pots occurring in the soil used to fill up the motte staircase ramp, to fill the space under the barbican tower floor and to level up the courtyard near the barbican bridge (**23b**). This suggests that soil was being brought from a single ditch or quarry source. The architectural evidence has already been mentioned. It is the combination of distinctive masons' marks, characteristic tooling and fine sculptured stonework details that enables the archaeologist to identify the contemporary work, especially the fine ashlar technique used on the revetted and chamfered bases around the barbican tower and the staircase drum towers (**20**, **21**).

The third phase (numbered 5b in the detailed excavation report) represents the occupation and regular use of the three main areas of the castle: keep, barbican and courtyard domestic ranges. Again dating is imprecise but it must cover the decades 1270–1350. This spans the later years of John the seventh earl (died 1304), who was frequently campaigning with the king in Wales and Scotland, and the troubled occupancy by his grandson John the eighth earl (died 1347). Indeed the archaeological material cannot be so neatly categorised and a general occupation period runs from about 1270 to about 1400 (**23c**). This means that as well as the de Warenne occupation, there is also the episode of Lancaster's tenancy 1317–26 and of the quasi-royal ownership 1347–1400. The latter period is discussed in the next chapter, but the private war might be expected to leave some trace in the archaeological record. However apart from a repair on the south wall of the keep, which may just be an alteration to put in a garderobe shaft, and an intermittent destruction layer on the south side of the bailey, there is no clear evidence; what there is cannot be closely dated except to say that it is in this phase and is of fourteenth-century date. This may mean that the change of ownership from de Warenne to Lancaster was peaceful or that such skirmishing as there was took place well away from Sandal castle. There is certainly no evidence for a total rebuilding of the castle, as the Victorian excavator Dr. Walker believed he had found. Admittedly there is ample indication of fourteenth-century stonework, but these pieces tend to be chimneys and cornices which might either be late in the building's completion or else be exposed details needing early replacement because of the poor quality of the stone initially used. This repair may well have been coupled with a desire for more elaborate detail and a display of wealth as befitted a duke's residence. There is also good evidence that some of the window glass was of early fourteenth-century designs, but again this is insufficient grounds for arguing that there was wholesale renewal.

War in West Yorkshire

Even though the "war" of 1317 and the Lancastrian occupation is elusive in archaeological material, the episode does have one bonus in the documentary record. In March 1322 the rebellious Thomas of Lancaster was defeated at the battle of Boroughbridge, brought captive to his castle at Pontefract, tried and found guilty of treason before a panel of his fellow barons and then executed on a hill just north of Pontefract. His treason meant that his possessions were forfeited to the crown and Edward II took immediate steps to discover what the earl possessed in his various castles and manors. A royal official, William de la Beche, was installed at Sandal as its constable for five days to make a spot check of the castle's contents. These contents comprised what he actually found belonging to the castle, what had been seized from a Lancastrian supporter Henry de Suthill at nearby Darton and what had been brought in by "plunderers" employed by the king to take livestock from Lancastrian sympathisers. When William's task was completed and his account had been submitted, he handed the castle over to Thomas Deyville who acted as keeper for the next six-month period March to September 1322. In many respects the two accounts are complementary in that the same list of goods is checked, handed over and received, but it is possible to see Thomas selling the unwanted goods or sending animals to other manors where they could be put to better use.

During William's period as constable there are three elements to his accounts: what he sold, what he spent and what he handed over. He sells surplus food, namely wheat, oats, wine, beef, bacon, herrings and salt; he also sells off surplus livestock (a colt and seven oxen), the hides of three cavalry horses which had died of disease, six pieces of iron and a valuable lady's saddle. He spends money on necessary supplies and services. Hay and fodder are bought for the horses and cattle. Payments are made to a smith for shoeing horses, to a locksmith for providing new locks throughout the castle and to workmen for repairing the castle roofs. Six persons are paid for looking after the castle: William de la Beche and his squire, a janitor (porter) and a watchman, and a forester and his boy looking after the park around the castle. William receives and hands over the provisions within the castle, presumably in the cellars; these consist of wheat, oats, rye and peas, together with barrels or tuns of wine. Other food supplies were in the larder — carcases of beef, sides of bacon, casks of herring and measures of salt. The livestock is carefully listed together with its origin whether castle stock or captured goods: different types of horses and cattle only are mentioned, presumably because sheep, pigs and deer were allowed to roam freely. The castle's armoury is carefully listed. It represents rather a motley collection. The personal armour includes 13 helmets, mainly bascinets, protection in plate armour for neck, chest and legs together with 23 worn-out quilted underjackets; there are hand weapons of 71 lances and 8 hand-bows, 11 shields or targes and one iron mantlet for protection in siege warfare. Two types of catapult are listed; four bolt-throwing ballista with 200 iron bolts lacking their pointed heads and one arrow-throwing springald with 60 arrows for it; there are cranking handles for both types of machine and also two dismantled war-machines. Two canvas tents with horse-hair guy ropes are a reminder that armies had to be ready to campaign in all weathers. The smith's supplies included 39 pieces of iron and 327 cart nails or "strakes". The kitchen furniture included a variety of bronze pots and cauldrons, two iron spits, two iron firedogs, two wooden buckets, three washing troughs and two pairs of hand-mills or querns. The cellar contents are listed as 12 iron barrels, 8 empty wine tuns, 3 casks, 7 barrels for ale and 6 vats.

The domestic furniture comprised eight tables with straw-padded settles, a chest and two cupboards or "hutches", while a cask for receiving alms presumably stood in the chapel. Apart from the larder no specific rooms are mentioned in William's survey. One must also assume that a lot of the private furniture such as clothes chests and spice hampers was brought from castle to castle, much in the same way as land-owning families at the start of this century packed up and sent off the linen, clothing and cutlery when they travelled up to Scotland for the grouse shooting and the deer stalking. Having made his list William then moved on to undertake a similar task at Dolforwyn in mid Wales where Roger Mortimer's castle was forfeited through treason.

His successor Thomas Deyville took over the contents intact but began to dispose of unwanted provisions and livestock. Of the wheat, rye, peas and oats, only the oats was kept as seed for planting and the remainder sold though some had been kept too long and been attacked by rats and mice or gone mouldy. Much of the wine was sold but some had gone putrid. The beef, bacon and herrings were part consumed, part sold and part continued to be kept in storage. Of the livestock the horses were stabled at the home farm or grange, the mares were grazed in the adjacent forest and the colts were sent for the king's use. Seventeen cows, two oxen and a bull were restored to the lands of Henry de Suthill; presumably he was now pardoned. Most of the bullocks went to the king's use and one anticipates were soon eaten. A few of the oxen were kept at Sandal to work the farmlands, while the main stock of cows and bullocks was sent to the cattle ranch in Sowerbyshire in the Pennine heights of Wakefield Manor. At the end of Thomas Deyville's period as keeper the next year's harvest had been gathered in and the farm stock had increased by the birth of foals and calves. The next custodian was Richard Moseley but no detailed accounts survive of his stewardship. In many ways the two accounts just discussed are typical of other castle "inventories". The possessions are a mixture of useful and ancient goods; the livestock and farm produce is the regular mainstay of the baronial economy.

Food and drink

Only a small part of this account is reflected in the archaeological record. None of the lanceheads, arrowheads or plate armour can be dated as early as this phase (see **45 d–f**); none of the listed kitchen equipment has survived, though one might expect the querns or "pairs of mills" to have been discarded when worn out just as the stone bowls of the kitchen mortars have been. It is the considerable quantity of animal bone dumped in the ditch around the barbican that provides material comparable to the documentary record (**24:** phase 5). The 2,218 bone fragments represent 5% of the entire bone deposit from within the castle. Although dog, hare, rabbit, chicken, goose and other fowl have been identified, the bulk of the animal bone is of deer (39.5%), cow (31%), sheep (15.5%), pig (10.5%) and horse (3.5%). The deer, both fallow and red, is at the highest proportion of this phase and in the succeeding period, implying a well-managed park and forest, certainly more than the 30 acres of deer pasture mentioned in the 1304 survey (**38**). Cattle gradually increase in importance as a food animal throughout the medieval occupation of the castle, as the surrounding woodland was cleared. Sheep and pig remain at a relatively low level as a food source in this phase and the following period up to 1450. There is documentary evidence in the

Table 1

The number of bone fragments from each phase

Phase	*Date*	*No of fragments*	*% of total sample*
7	1106–1130	1,957	4.8
6	c1130–c1240	996	2.5
5	c1240–c1400	2,218	5.5
4	c1400–c1450	2,103	5.2
3	c1450–1484	3,371	8.3
2	1484–5	7,716	19.1
1	1485–c1600	15,743	38.8
+	1645	6,381	15.7
total		40,485	99.9

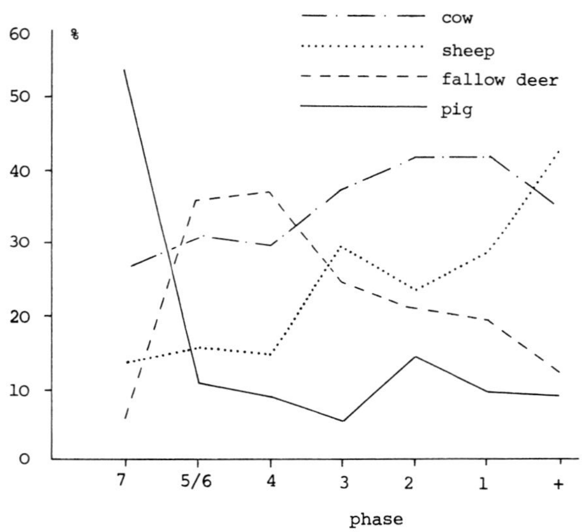

24. Graph showing proportions of animal bone from each phase of occupation

1304 survey for a small fish-pond near the castle which was unusable because the fish died and a large fish-pond of $4\frac{1}{2}$ acres using the mill dam in the valley below the castle, presumably at Milnthorpe. However there has been no archaeological evidence for the bones of freshwater fish such as carp, bream or pike, but only the bones of cod which must have been caught in the North Sea. Two types of shell fish, oyster and mussel, occur in this period and must also represent long distance trade.

Daily life

The other types of archaeological evidence vary in their usefulness. The coin evidence is modest. Two coins of Edward I were lost in the area between the main gatehouse and the Privy Chamber, an area occupied by a barn and workshop at this phase but later occupied by the Constable's Lodgings. A third coin of this king, dating to 1282–3 and lost when nearly new, was found among the earliest dumping in the barbican ditch. Two other coins of Edward I came from the upper levels within the barbican ditch and, though obviously disturbed, do indicate the intensity of occupation when these coins were in common use. The evidence of daily life is similarly scarce, hinting at a high standard of cleanliness within the occupied buildings or pointing at the disposal of rubbish on the paddocks and fields outside the castle ditches. A ring of silver, a few small items of bronze and an ornate bronze thimble are all that occurs at this phase, though the barbican ditch contains evidence of bronze casting using small ingots and of iron working, presumably using iron from local sources such as Emley and Bretton.

The pottery evidence in this phase is extensive: 2585 sherds (2090 in the barbican ditch) representing at least 629 different vessels (**23c**). The vessel forms display the same range as before, mainly jugs and jars with far fewer bowls and a single example of a handled ladle; there are no curfews but some fragmentary vessels of unusual forms cannot be immediately determined as to their original shape and purpose. A new form is the narrow cylindrical drinking jug probably made at Cowick in the Humber basin. There is also a pottery copy of the two handled metal cauldron common in the fourteenth century. This vessel is a reminder that many pottery vessels were accompanied in use at kitchen and at table by a range of bronze and iron pans, leather bottles and wooden bowls. Usually only the evidence of the pottery survives archaeologically, while in the documentary record only the higher value of the bronze and iron vessels is noted and the rest are ignored. When they were worn out the bronze and iron vessels could be used as scrap and be melted down by the smiths, thereby disappearing from the archaeological evidence. However when pottery was broken there was no further use for it and it was discarded in and around the castle.

The range of pottery fabrics is much more extensive than before with 25 different fabrics occurring in the lowest level of the barbican ditch. The local gritty wares predominate but there is a far greater range of fine wares and of varied Humber wares. The two new themes are the introduction of purple wares and also of purple glazes on red bodies, and secondly the presence of two sherds of Rhineland stoneware from Langerwehe occurring before 1400 though not necessarily before 1350. The jugs now have a more varied or experimental colour range in their glazes and tend to be more ornately decorated with a combination of combing, notching, applied strips and discs. Sometimes the bases of the jugs are separately made which assists in the attachment of handles to narrow necked jugs before the base is sealed on. It is possible that some distinctive stamps may be a guide to the work of individual potters.

Three fabrics from beyond Yorkshire are encountered in the barbican ditch deposit and throw light on the wider aspects of the administrative history of Sandal. Another sherd of Grimston ware continues the association with Castle Acre which was only broken in 1347. Four sherds of West Sussex ware may well point to vessels brought from Lewes, the principal seat of the de Warenne earls of Surrey. A single body sherd from an Oxfordshire-type jug prompts an interesting proposal from Stephen Moorhouse in his detailed pottery report. He suggests that this jug reached Sandal through the Buckinghamshire holdings of Henry de la Walda, an early fourteenth-century steward of the manor of Wakefield who had extensive property at Wing in that county. The origin of these different fabrics can show links which might be suspected from the tenurial background of the widespread estates. The distribution of vessels within Sandal castle can show links between different buildings which were in use at the same time. Similar vessels occur in the lowest level of the barbican ditch, in the kitchen, in the bakehouse and upon the courtyard surface near the bailey well where there was a barn and industrial workshop. This linking of contemporary zones of occupation can be shown just as convincingly as has been the case with other earlier distributions. The potential for information derived from pottery studies is considerable and further lines of enquiry are being developed every year.

This chapter has examined the building of the stone castle and the first century of its occupation. The evidence can show in some detail how the castle was built and what standard of life was attained. Yet there are other aspects which archaeological approaches cannot illuminate; wall foundations might support two, three or four floor-levels in a tower — certainty is almost impossible; the frequently-cleaned floor will not be as informative about the details of daily life as the ill-kept household where food remains and pottery were trodden into a mud floor and where small coins and minute items of jewelry were never recovered when dropped and lost. Equally there are aspects of daily life on which the documentary record is silent. Do the account rolls of the manor of Wakefield start in 1274 only because in that year building at the castle was sufficiently finished for the account clerk to move into his office? Does the keeper's account of 1322 mention only six paid officials because that is the total that were needed to run the estate or because the rest of the household had income from other local sources? Many other questions are prompted by the tantalising hints in the documents just as there are similar questions arising from the variable survival of the material evidence. Only when we can study the castle in Richard III's reign or in the Civil War siege do the two strands of evidence become at all abundant and the detective story easier to follow.

Sandal under the Dukes of York and the Yorkist Kings

Edward III had a large and ambitious family to provide for; his sons needed estates and titles in keeping with their rank as princes of blood royal; his daughters needed dowries to sweeten their marriages to foreign royalty. The death of John de Warenne in 1347 provided the king with an excellent opportunity to increase the estates of his fifth son Edmund of Langley. Sandal and the manor of Wakefield along with other holdings of the de Warennes north of the Trent stayed with Edmund and his descendants for 125 years through four generations.

In addition to Sandal and Conisbrough Edmund of Langley held estates at Stamford and Grantham and from 1362 enjoyed the title of Earl of Cambridge, a dignity previously bestowed on his maternal uncle. His prospects were improved by marriage to Isabella, coheiress of Castile and Leon in northern Spain. Her ancestor had married Edward I and her sister Constance was married to Edmund's elder brother John of Gaunt. While John exercised a vigorous political role nationally, and also built up his Yorkshire estates based on Pontefract and Knaresborough, Edmund played a less effective moderating role in the disputes at the end of Edward III's reign and during his nephew Richard II's troubled reign. In an aggressive militaristic society at war with France and at odds with the peasantry at home, moderation was seen as weakness. However Edmund campaigned regularly in France and Portugal with his father and brothers, and was rewarded with the castle of Wark on Tweed on the Scottish border. A more welcome grant was of Fotheringay in northern Northamptonshire in 1377, and Edmund and his heirs made it their favourite castle and estate centre.

As a reward for Edmund's support for Richard II he was created duke of York in 1385. This elevation recognised the extensive estates Edmund held in Yorkshire and for the next hundred years Sandal's destiny was inseparable from the Yorkist family. The new duke played an ambiguous role in the latter years of Richard II's reign, acting as Regent on three occasions during the king's absence abroad but later was prepared to welcome another younger nephew Henry of Bolingbroke when he bid for the crown. On Edmund's death in 1402 his more militant but politically untrustworthy eldest son Edward became duke. Much of his time was spent campaigning in Ireland and he was made military commander with the title Constable of England. He also added buildings to Fotheringay castle and founded a college of priests at the church there. Edward's death during the battle of Agincourt (1415) and his brother Richard of Conisbrough's execution for treason at Southampton two months earlier, just before the invasion fleet sailed to France, brought the title to Edward's nephew Richard (Plantagenet) at the age of four.

There is nothing in this rehearsal of events to suggest that Sandal received more favoured attention than any other ducal estate. Indeed such documentation as survives and the pattern of granting official posts elsewhere through royal patronage indicate that Sandal and the manor of Wakefield were left in the hands of constables or stewards. They conducted local administration, protected the duke's hunting rights in the parks, made necessary repairs to buildings and ensured that manorial rights were enforced. There is evidence that the duke's step-mother, the widowed Maud (née Clifford), resided at Conisbrough and Sandal until her death in 1446. The duke may occasionally have visited his northern estates but he was generally involved in campaigns abroad until 1450. In all this there was little change from the situation under John de Warenne, the last earl of that line.

The fifteenth century was a troubled time for the English monarchy. The military victories of Henry V in France had brought wealth and prestige to the crown but the marriage of Henry to Catherine of Valois implanted the seeds of mental instability in their son Henry VI just as it had afflicted her father Charles VI. So long as Henry V's brother John duke of Bedford ruled in the young king's name the possessions in France could be held, albeit with difficulty. John's death left the king at the mercy of rival factions. One of these was led by Richard duke of York. Richard (Plantagenet) could claim through his father's marriage to Anne (Mortimer) to be descended from Edward III's third son Lionel, while Henry VI was only descended from the fourth son, John of Gaunt. It was a chain of descent exactly similar to that used by Edward III to justify his own claim to the French crown. Additonally Richard was of the third generation in descent from Edward III and over ten years senior in age, while Henry VI was of the fourth generation. However for many years Richard was kept away from court and from royal councils by being given military commands in France and Ireland but provided with insufficient funds or men to enable him to gain success and prestige in his campaigns.

Richard of York and the Battle of Wakefield

Not until spring 1450 was Richard permanently based in England. He then played an active role in politics and tried to reform the biased and expensive government conducted by minor household officials acting in the king's name at the bidding of his queen Margaret of Anjou. During the next decade Richard of York and his supporters armed themselves and fought to secure control of the king's person; to do so would enable them to govern in his name. These early battles and confrontations took place on the approaches to London, as at St. Albans (1455), or on the Welsh borderland, as at Ludford bridge (1459). They ushered in a period of political turmoil in which strong local magnates fortified their castles and gathered together armed bands of retainers to overawe their tenants.

Early in 1460 Richard of York returned from exile in Ireland and made his only serious attempt to displace Henry and occupy the throne for himself. After the battle of Northampton in July had placed the king under his control, Richard claimed the crown at a council in October. However his action was greeted without enthusiasm and Richard had to settle for the title of "Protector and heir apparent". In December the duke of York rode north to punish Lancastrian nobles who with the connivance of Margaret of Anjou were harrassing his tenants. It was an irony of Edward III's gifts to his sons that the Lancastrian inheritance based on Pontefract, Knaresborough and Clitheroe was so closely interwoven with the Yorkist ancestral lands based on Conisbrough and Sandal. Elsewhere the Lancastrian earldom of Leicester was within striking distance of the Yorkist lands at Fotheringay; the Yorkist castle of Anstey in Hertfordshire controlled one route to the north and their castle at Stamford controlled another.

Richard of York's punitive campaign ended in disaster. He had come north with insufficient troops to complete his task and was trapped in Sandal castle by Lancastrian forces based at Pontefract. On December 30th the Lancastrians attacked a foraging party sent into the park from Sandal. This encounter was watched from the castle towers and the duke of York impetuously marched his forces towards Wakefield to assist the foragers. As Richard did this, the main body of the Lancastrian army under Lord Clifford, which had been hidden in ambush at Milnthorpe, advanced between the river and the castle, thereby cutting off any retreat back to the castle. The Lancastrians engaged the duke's army driving them towards Wakefield. The castle which had been left lightly guarded was soon captured by a small detachment under the command of James Butler, earl of Wiltshire. The main battle was fought on Wakefield Green, now known as Manygates Lane and Portobello. The duke was mortally wounded. Nearly half of the 3000 men led by the duke are said to have perished in the battle and were buried in the fields. When the foundations of Portobello House were dug in 1825 human bones, broken swords, spurs and fragments of armour were found. The duke's head was cut off on the orders of Lord Clifford; it was taken to York and placed above Micklegate Bar, symbolically decorated with a crown of paper and straw. Richard's second son Edmund, earl of Rutland, then a youth of seventeen, was also killed by Lord Clifford on Wakefield Bridge and his head was displayed at York on a pole beside his father's head.

The death of Richard duke of York brought possession of Sandal, the manor of Wakefield and the entire Yorkist inheritance into the hands of his more resolute and militarily skilful elder son Edward, earl of March. His first victory was on the Welsh borderland at Mortimer's Cross in February 1461 and in the following month he proclaimed himself king as Edward IV. At the end of March Edward decisively defeated the Lancastrian army in a snowstorm at Towton near Tadcaster. Among the dead was Lord Clifford whose head replaced that of Richard on the gates of York. As a memorial to his father and the fallen at Wakefield Edward IV erected a cross on the spot where his father had died on the west side of Manygates Lane. It was demolished by Parliamentary soldiers in 1645 during the siege of the castle. A replacement memorial column in the form of a Gothic pinnacle was erected on the same spot in 1897 and can still be seen in the grounds of Manygates School. A further act of generosity by Edward was to endow the existing chapel on Wakefield Bridge so that prayers might be said for the souls of the fallen. A similar commemoration was made at Towton where a new chapel was built and a chaplain funded so that he could say masses for the benefit of the dead buried on the battlefield and at nearby Saxton.

A royal castle

After the battles of Wakefield and Towton the course of national events moved away from Yorkshire. Henry VI and his queen Margaret of Anjou fled to Scotland. The new king visited his northern lands only occasionally; he stopped on his way to parliaments held at York or rested when he was marching north to fight the Scots punishing them for their support of the Lancastrian king. However Edward now had a far greater choice of castles to accommodate him and his household. There were the Yorkist castles of Sandal and Conisbrough; there were the Lancastrian castles of Pontefract, Knaresborough and Haverah Park; and there were the royal castles of York, Scarborough, Pickering and Tickhill (**25**). It is not surprising that Sandal saw little of the new ruler.

Edward's reign was not without its difficulties. He was forced to seek exile in Burgundy in 1470 but returned in March 1471 landing at the mouth of the Humber and staying at Sandal on his route south. He marched on London and regained the crown, defeating the Lancastrians at Barnet. He may have made further occasional visits, but the castle at Sandal was regularly inspected by the king's financial officers, his receiver and surveyor for the duchy of York or for the counties beyond the Trent. The castle constable and principal local officer was Sir John Savile of Thornhill who died at Sandal in 1482. The death of Edward IV in the following year and the usurpation by his brother Richard as king mark

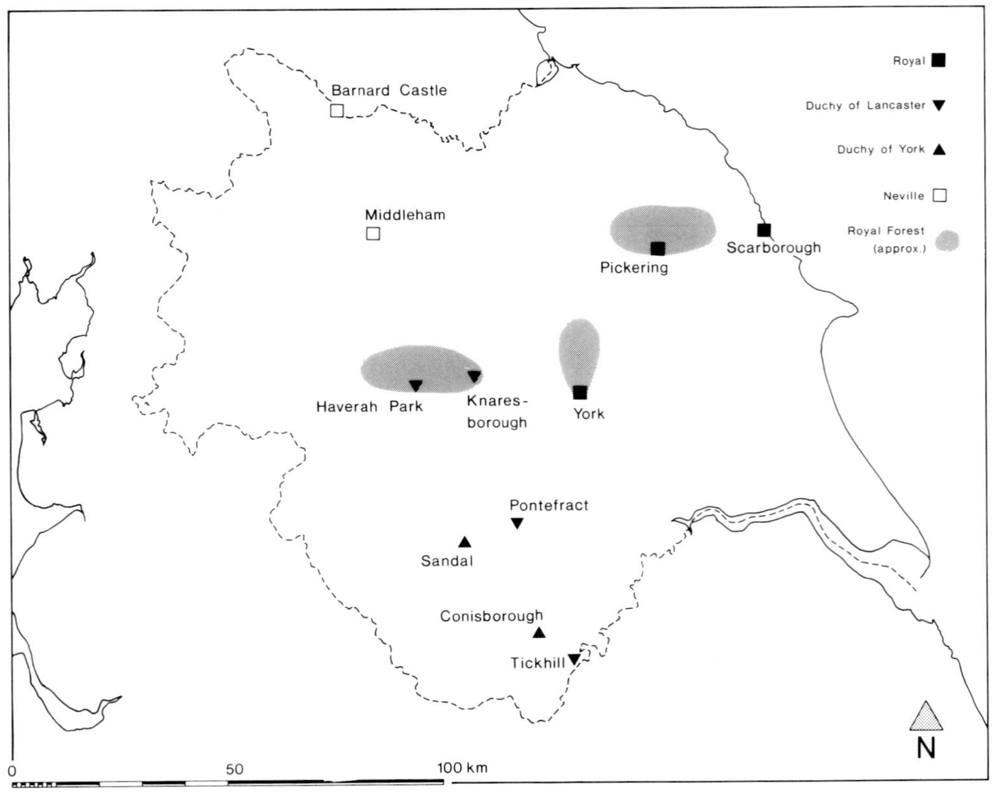

25. Map of royal castles in Yorkshire (1460–1485)

:s. The school was very
l by him; the children
obtaining scholarships.
pointment to the High
Mr. John Gurr was ap-
astership, and ably con-
to the time of his death.
as the next headmaster,
chool kept up its repu-
nd for obtaining scholar-
Stewart was appointed
Wellesley Street school,
illiam N. McIntosh, the
ho conducted the Epsom
success for eleven years,
cceed him. Under Mr.
ent the school has fully
n in every respect. The
on the point of erecting
lding with class-rooms,
d on the most scientific
ol has a flag staff with
ining the names of the
eers and civilians, who
South Africa, from One-
Its cost was subscribed
en, the Onehunga Rifles,
ire Brigade.

cINTOSH, the Headmas-
ga Public School, is a
He joined the Auckland
1880, and was appointed
n in 1896. Mr. McIntosh
unders of the Onehunga
is captain.

IURCH, Onehunga. This
e oldest in the diocese of

as the school, was erected as early as 1850, and replaced by the present building in 1877. It is situated in Grey Street, Onehunga, and can accommodate 250 persons. An efficient choir, under the leadership of Mr. J. Laking, is assisted by an American organ. The Onehunga church is the headquarters of the Manukau circuit, in which there are four other churches; namely, Otahuhu, Mangere, Woodside and Flat Bush. The Sunday school recently erected is one of the best appointed buildings of the kind to be found in the Auckland district. It comprises a large assembly hall with six class-rooms besides adequate provision for the duties of the secretary and librarian. Here the work of the school, Christian Endeavour Society and Band of Hope is vigorously carried out. The parsonage, which adjoins the church, is an historical dwelling, built at Mangungu, Hokianga, in 1839, for the late Rev. Mr. Bumby, a pioneer missionary, and removed to its present site in 1856.

THE REV. CORNELIUS GRIFFIN, who succeeded the Rev. S. Lawry in the charge of the Onehunga Wesleyan Church, was ordained to the ministry with Mr. Lawry at Nelson. Mr. Griffin was born in Birmingham, and became a probationer at Bedford. Arriving in New Zealand in 1879, he went to Auckland, and the Waikato, where he was stationed for about two years, during which he was ordained at Nelson, which he visited for the purpose. Mr. Griffin ministered at Waimate, Lawrence, Greymouth, Hokitika, Invercargill, Springston, and Leeston, prior to taking up his present charge.

Rev. SAMUEL LAWRY, formerly Minis

20.3.23.

SIR JOHN SAVILLE OF THORNHILL D. 1482 SANDAL

SEE PAGE 52. "SANDAL CASTLE"

(POSSIBLE CONNECTION TO HASELDINES c1450)

a critical point in Sandal's use and are best dealt with in a separate section (below page 62).

The bare record of historical events portrays a castle in occasional residence by its ducal owners or their family but it is a stronghold permanently garrisoned and occupying a major role in local affairs. It is necessary now to see how far the architectural and archaeological evidence supports or enlarges upon this record.

Decoration and Comfort at Sandal

It must be admitted that there is no clear evidence at ground level for structural alterations to the castle's buildings except in the area closest to the gatehouse. What does survive are numerous fragments of sculptured stone and painted window glass which indicate an increased adornment of the bailey buildings and, to a much lesser extent, those of the keep. Although the majority of the carved stonework is of fourteenth-century date and is likely to be from doorways, window openings and vaulting of the Warenne period, it is equally clear that work on the castle continued during the greater part of the fifteenth century. The evidence comes from the jambs or sides of a doorway, an arch from a door head, the panels of an internal screen and the ribs of a stone vault. It is not known to which rooms these pieces belonged. One fragment of considerable size which can be identified is a studded bulbous finial. This is almost certainly the cap from the Lodging Chamber turret; it is shown on the 1562 drawing (**36**) with an overlarge fleur-de-lys termination. This same fleur-de-lys badge was adopted as the arms of Wakefield on its seal and on its heraldic coat.

Of greater interest is the evidence of decoration to the buildings provided by the smaller pieces of sculpture. Three stones are of particular interest. The first is a knight's head with a fierce grin; the head is protected by chain mail and the brow is wreathed by a head band of alternating suns and roses, a Yorkist badge. The forward thrust of the head suggests that the carving was positioned on a decorative stringcourse or as a stop on a door arch. Another possibility is that it was a warrior sentinel guarding the battlements. Such warriors were carved at many northern castles such as Middleham in Wensleydale, Alnwick and Belsay in Northumberland and on the gates of York. The chain mail suggests a date before 1400 but often the figures were carved in older styles. The second interesting carving is a water spout or gargoyle in the form of a grotesque head with a bulbous ape-like face and a ribbed headdress. This is the type of grotesque face that decorates the margins of psalters and books of devotion; it is probably early fifteenth century. The third and most attractive carving is on a fine-grained pale fawn sandstone. It is part of a gargoyle spout in the form of a falcon (**26**); the feathers are delicately depicted and the curve of the wings is carefully modelled. The sculpture was found in the moat between the keep and the barbican; it may well have slid down the motte slope from a position on one of the keep's towers. The use of falcons, as a distinctive symbol of the Yorkist family, is to be seen on the King's Beasts carved for Edward IV on St. George's chapel at Windsor and on King's College chapel at Cambridge, but it was introduced much earlier as a badge.

The falcon occurs on five pieces of painted glass, three from the barbican ditch and two from the keep (**27**). One piece has well-drawn feathers but on two others the feathers are more schematically drawn. Three pieces show bells on the

26. The falcon sculpture showing breast and wing (the head was on the right)

falcon's legs. The falcon was the principal heraldic beast of the house of York, being shown with wings closed on the early seal of Edmund of Langley (in about 1360) and appearing with bells on the legs on the seal of Richard of York who died in 1460. Only after 1471 does Edward IV adopt the badge of a silver falcon with wings partly outstretched and perched within an iron chain loop or "fetterlock". Another piece of glass may show the seated white hind, a badge of Richard II which was also used by Edmund of Langley. Yet another heraldic beast was the white dog or talbot shown on two pieces of glass from the barbican ditch (**27e**). The only occasion when the talbot may have been used was in a brief period when Edward IV was betrothed to Eleanor, daughter of John Talbot, first earl of Shrewsbury, and in an equally brief period of 15 months when John's son was constable of the castle between 1459 and 1461. These and some other pieces of glass with religious scenes point to an attractively decorated castle during the early fifteenth century. The main structure of the castle was little changed but its standards of comfort and decoration were steadily increased.

The only part of the structure where there seems to have been new buildings was in the area between the Gatehouse and the Privy Chamber in the main courtyard close to the well (**28**). These underlay what later became the Constable's Lodgings. In the early fifteenth century (phase 4) there were two slightly built structures: the more southerly, room T, was set on low sleeper walls of stone and used the north wall of the Privy Chamber as one wall but had an east wall so that it did not abut the curtain wall. The more northerly shed, room P, was of timber built construction with its main posts set on sill stones or stylobates; the side walls could be identified but one end wall must have used the curtain wall and the other end wall was destroyed. The space between rooms P and T alongside the well does not appear to have had any building in it at this phase.

There are no finds of metalwork or coins that need to be particularly noted in the early fifteenth century, but the pottery has some interesting characteristics and provides evidence of building use not otherwise available. The greater part of

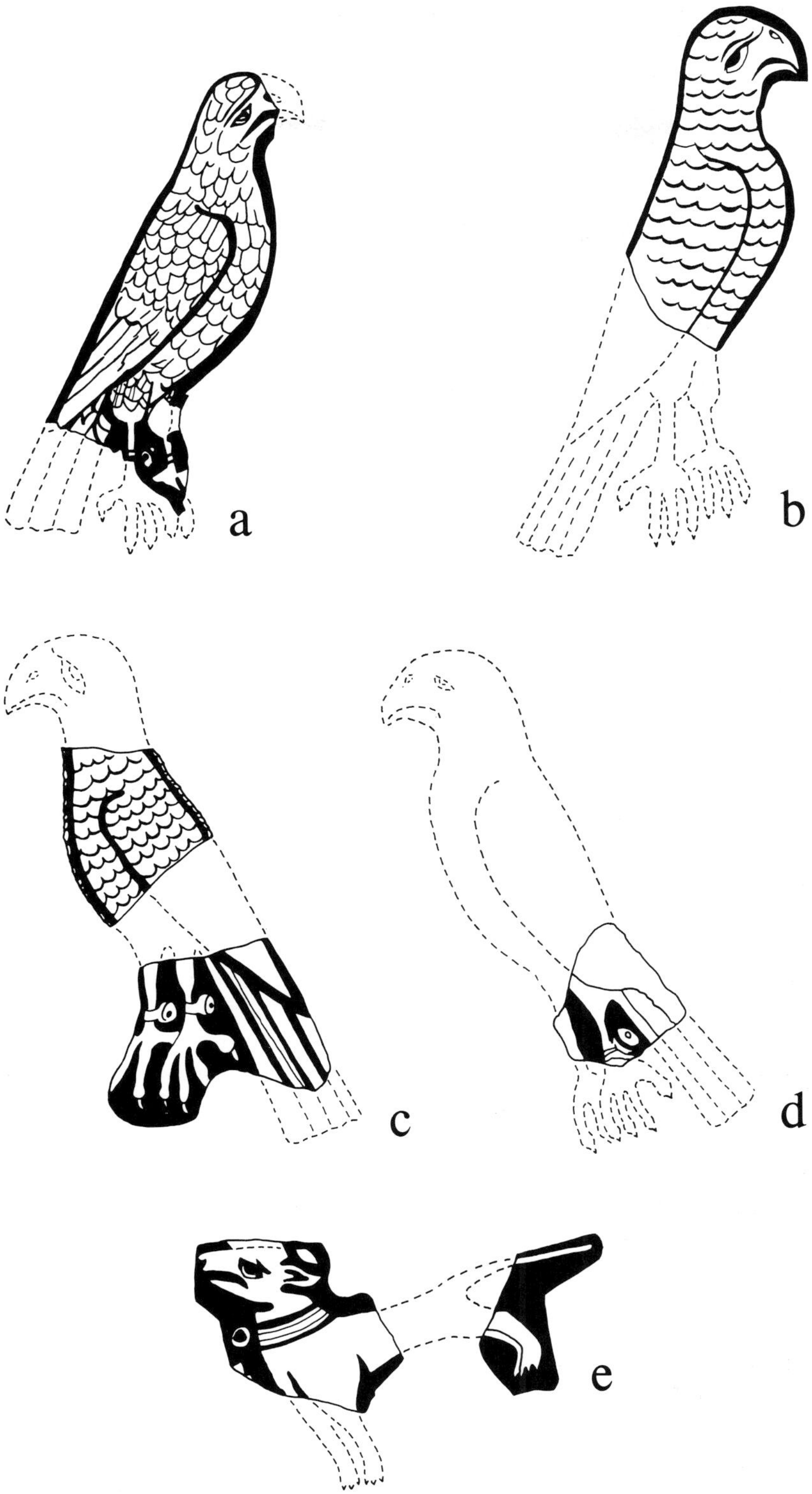

27. The heraldic window glass: falcons and talbot

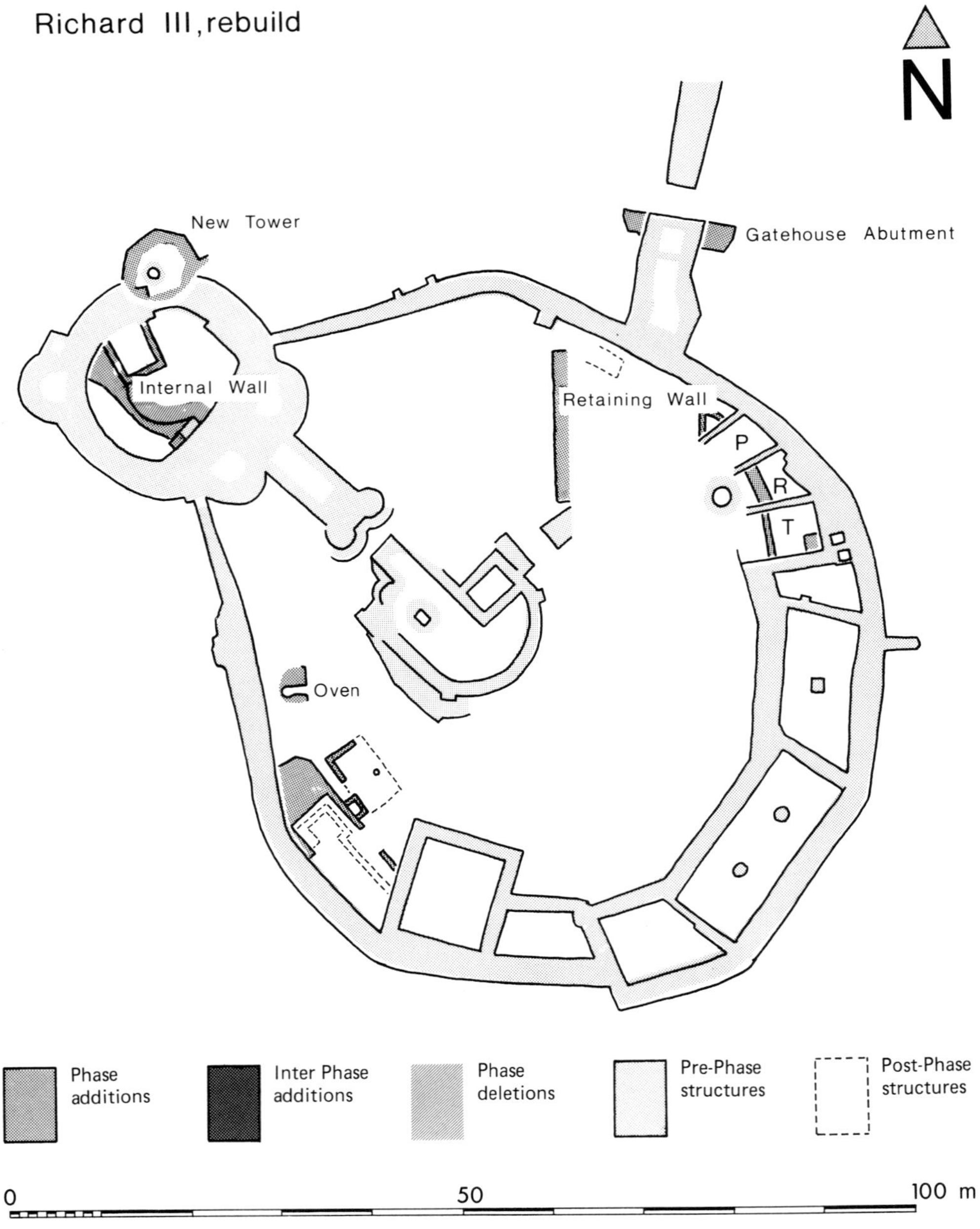

28. Plan of the stone castle: Richard III's new work

this evidence comes from the barbican ditch: it began to be filled during the fourteenth century but this process accelerated in the fifteenth century. The dumping in this ditch of a large number of near complete vessels, including a considerable deposit of pots used for industrial purposes, suggests that level 4 in the barbican ditch represents a clearance of the contents of the bailey buildings in the first half of the fifteenth century. It is useless to speculate upon the circumstances which prompted such a clearance, but a drastic change from a castle ticking over on a care-and-maintenance basis to a residence fully occupied by a ducal owner seems to be indicated. Some of the ceramic material is likely to have been in use for some decades when it was discarded and the bronze items of dress buckles and lace tags may equally have been lost many years before the clearance occurred.

This suggestion is borne out by the nature of the imported pottery which comes from both Spain and Germany. Although the southern wares are all in fragments there were Spanish lustreware jars from Valencia, drug jars or "albarellos" from the western Mediterranean and jugs or jars in decorated maiolica. These vessels, both painted and plain, suggest that there was a trade in attractive vessels imported for their appearance and a parallel trade in containers filled with spices imported for their contents. The German stonewares were often more complete, being either jugs or cups from Langerwehe in the Rhineland. These were presumably imported in the early fifteenth century to provide hard-wearing drinking vessels.

The range of local pottery fabrics and forms suggests kiln sources near Wakefield as well as at (or imitating) the products of Rawmarsh in south Yorkshire. The fabrics are mainly gritty wares with pale green glazes, sandy and soapy fabrics with a range of green and orange glazes and the hard fabrics of "Midland purple" wares. Many of the fabrics are of very general distribution throughout the eastern Pennines and across to the Humber estuary, with only the stamped decoration on the pale green glazed jugs of the York fine wares being easily distinguishable. It is likely that most of the 2000 sherds from the barbican ditch at this phase came from local kilns, but so far no association of a distinctive fabric, an unusual vessel form, an excavated kiln and a named potting family has yet been possible at Sandal. The likelihood that kilns within the manor of Wakefield supplied much of the pottery is shown by the absence of pottery from Upper Heaton near Halifax which was on Fountains Abbey lands. The forms of the vessels show that the majority were for storage or for cooking: jugs and jars predominate, while other storage vessels are cisterns and tripod legged pitchers; cooking pots, bowls and dishes supplied the needs of the kitchen. Much fewer in number were pottery urinals and one example of a pottery curfew, of which insufficient survived to show whether it was semi-circular to cover overnight a wall hearth or fully circular to protect the embers of a centrally placed hearth.

The practice of alchemy

There were two areas within the castle bailey where industrial processes connected with the practice of alchemy may have taken place. The first is indicated by the evidence provided by 8 sherds in and around the gatehouse, giving only slight evidence that chemical processes took place on an upper floor of the gatehouse. Far firmer evidence is provided by pottery and glass in an area of the bailey courtyard in the angle of the kitchen and the larder. Here there was a hearth about a metre square with stone walls and a stone ledge upon which chemical vessels could have been placed; in the barbican ditch most closely adjacent to this hearth there were many fragments of pottery and glass vessels of distinctive form (**23d**). There were over 770 sherds of industrial wares, representing a minimum of 170 vessels; most were in a dull red fabric, unglazed and hard-fired in order to resist unduly high temperatures. Their forms were distinctive with 26 main types indicating that pottery cucurbits were placed in sand-filled bowls and surrounded by large jars which acted as mantles. In the cucurbit the ingredients were heated; the sand bed dispersed the heat more evenly and seems to be a common method in the later middle ages. The purpose of the mantle was to protect the craftsman from the intense heat generated by the fire and to concentrate the heat onto the chemical process being conducted within. A long slit in the mantle allowed the alembic spout to project during the distillation process and vent holes in the mantle and others in a presumed jar lid prevented a build-up of gases from a coal or wood fuelled fire. On top of the cucurbits would be placed alembics with the mouth and spout facing downwards so that the distillation of liquids could be collected easily in beakers or flasks. Both the alembics and the flasks were of glass (**29**); these occurred in some 200 pieces of

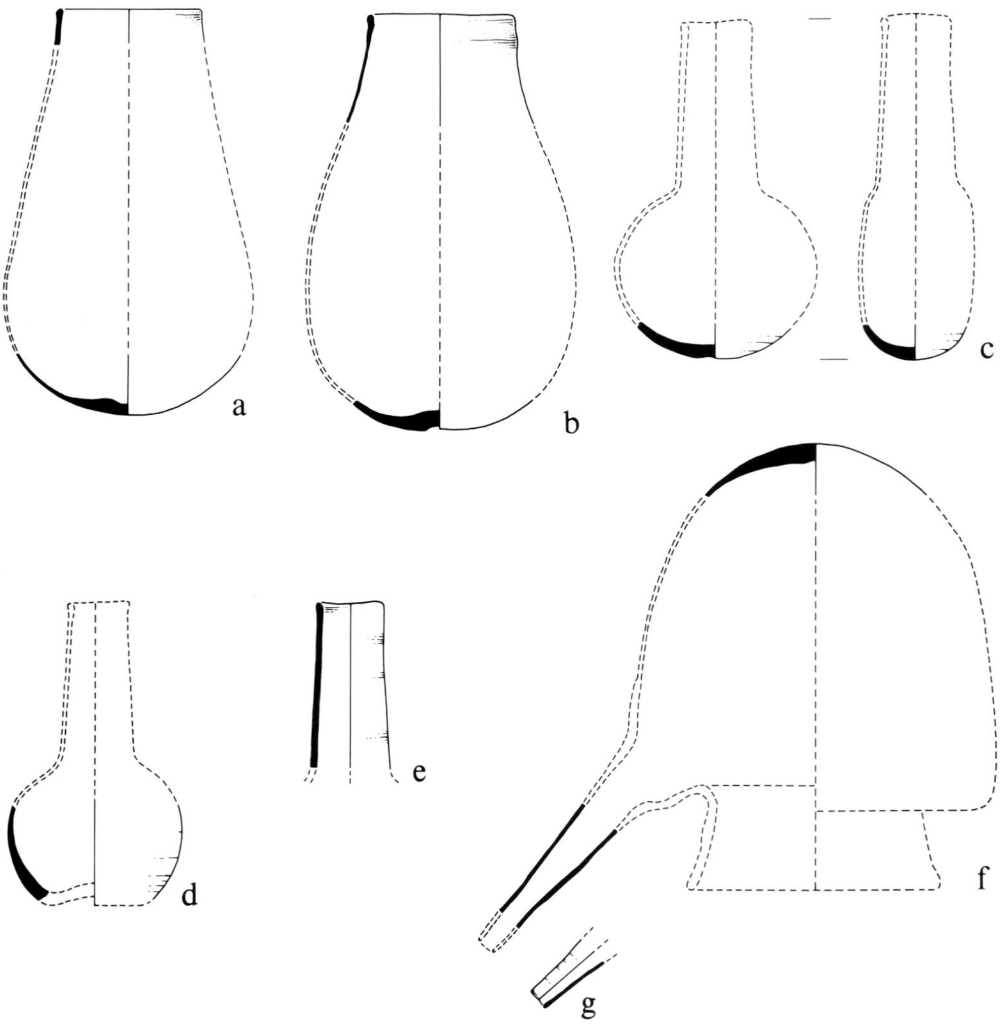

29. Glass vessels used in alchemy: flasks (a–e) and alembics (f–g).

vessel glass in the same area of deposit in the barbican ditch and represent the remains of at least 40 vessels of both recognisable and as yet unrecognised forms. Stephen Moorhouse in his reports on both the pottery and the glass stresses the importance of inspecting and interpreting both materials together. If the pottery had been sent off to a ceramic expert and the glass sent off to another museum expert, the significance of these industrial processes would not have been recognised and the use of the hearth in the bailey might not have been appreciated. In view of the fragile nature of the glass and the poor quality of its survival this is an important point to stress.

Without the integrated approach neither the location of the industrial workshop nor the nature of the processes would have been fully understood. Even so there are a number of uncertainties that cannot be satisfactorily resolved. It is uncertain whether there was any practice of alchemy in the gatehouse, but there is no other explanation for the deposit of industrial pottery in that area. Similarly although the hearth outside the larder was clearly used for the heating of industrial vessels (13 of which were found near it), there is no workshop in the bailey. Moorhouse was forced to conclude that the room where the alchemy was practised was on the first floor probably over the larder, close to the hearth and close to the biggest deposit of pottery and glass. It is still uncertain what substance or liquid was being produced or distilled. One possibility is a fairly prosaic chemical substance such as sulphur or arsenic; another is that it was the search for an elixir of youth or an acoholic spirit. There is no firm evidence on this point from the residues in the pottery cucurbit and there are no glass cucurbits surviving in reconstructable form. Until more research is completed one can only use the evidence of medieval alchemy recipe books to show what it was thought possible to produce by these methods.

Considerable space has been devoted to this discussion because it illustrates the way in which many different types of evidence have been brought together to understand one particular aspect of daily life at Sandal castle. It is only the thoroughness of the excavation and the complete examination of all the finds that permits such a reconstruction of the past to take place. In many castles there is relatively little evidence from the floors because these were paved or flagged and kept clean of all debris; there will be little stratified evidence from courtyard surfaces because these will be churned up with the passage of men and horses. There may even be little helpful material from the garderobes and wells because these would be cleaned out annually to ensure that the privies did not become a stinking health hazard and that the well water did not become contaminated by weed growth and dead vermin. Throughout the early fifteenth century at Sandal the major evidence of building use comes from the rubbish thrown into the barbican ditch and there is only minor occupation debris from within the bakehouse, within the keep, beneath the Constable's Lodging and on the courtyard surfaces.

The same pattern of information holds good for the next site phase (3) where the barbican ditch provides most of the clues to the occupation of the castle in the period 1450–1484. This is a time when Sandal must have been fully occupied. The pottery is little different in fabric or form from the previous half-century, but it is found in small fragments dispersed throughout one level in the barbican ditch. This is quite unlike the much larger numbers of near complete vessels deposited in distinct areas as parts of the castle were cleared out. In the case of the industrial vessels and glass these may point to a hasty disposal of the evidence, since it was illegal to practice alchemy without a royal warrant and no such licence relating to Sandal has been found on the Patent Rolls. This hints at an illegal enterprise by persons as yet unknown. Apart from the additional forms of handled ladle and chafing dish, a medieval version of plate warmer, there is a similar predominance of jugs and jars, an increase in cisterns for the storage and fermentation of beer and a decrease in cooking pots. Again it is necessary to realise that one sees only a portion, perhaps a half, of all the vessels used at the castle. The items of bronze and silver seldom get thrown away; items of iron can be melted down and recast; items of leather such as flasks and jugs will have perished; plates, platters and bowls of wood only survive in the exceptional circumstances of waterlogged conditions in wells, ditches and ponds; baskets and trays of wicker-work or plaited reeds will also have rotted away. The indestructible qualities of the pottery allow some reconstruction of daily life to be made but the limitations of the evidence must also be recognised.

The metalwork is also the result of random losses, mostly dumped in the barbican ditch and probably some distance from where they were used or discarded, but they do indicate the high quality of equipment used at the castle. The finest item is a gold finger ring (**30**) inscribed "tout le vostre" ("All yours") between plant ornament, perhaps rosemary; all the inlaid areas of plant and inscription are highlighted in white enamel. A similar finger ring engraved with three saints was picked up on the battlefield site; its inscription hidden against the wearer's flesh was "Pur bon amour" ("For good love" or "In true love"). Another delicate item was a bronze rose ornament (**31c**) found in a garderobe fill; this may have come from a button or a badge, and it is tempting to see it as part of a servant's livery with Yorkist emblems. A third item of higher than average workmanship is the bronze chape which terminated the end of a dagger scabbard and protected the leather from wear (**31f**). An indication of piety or superstition is the miniature pilgrim flask of cast lead (**31g**); this is in the form of a leather purse with one face ribbed in imitation of a scallop shell and the plainer side marked with the letter "J". There seems no doubt that it is a pilgrim souvenir containing holy water brought back from the shrine of St. James at Compostella

30. A gold finger-ring, showing the word "tout" (all)

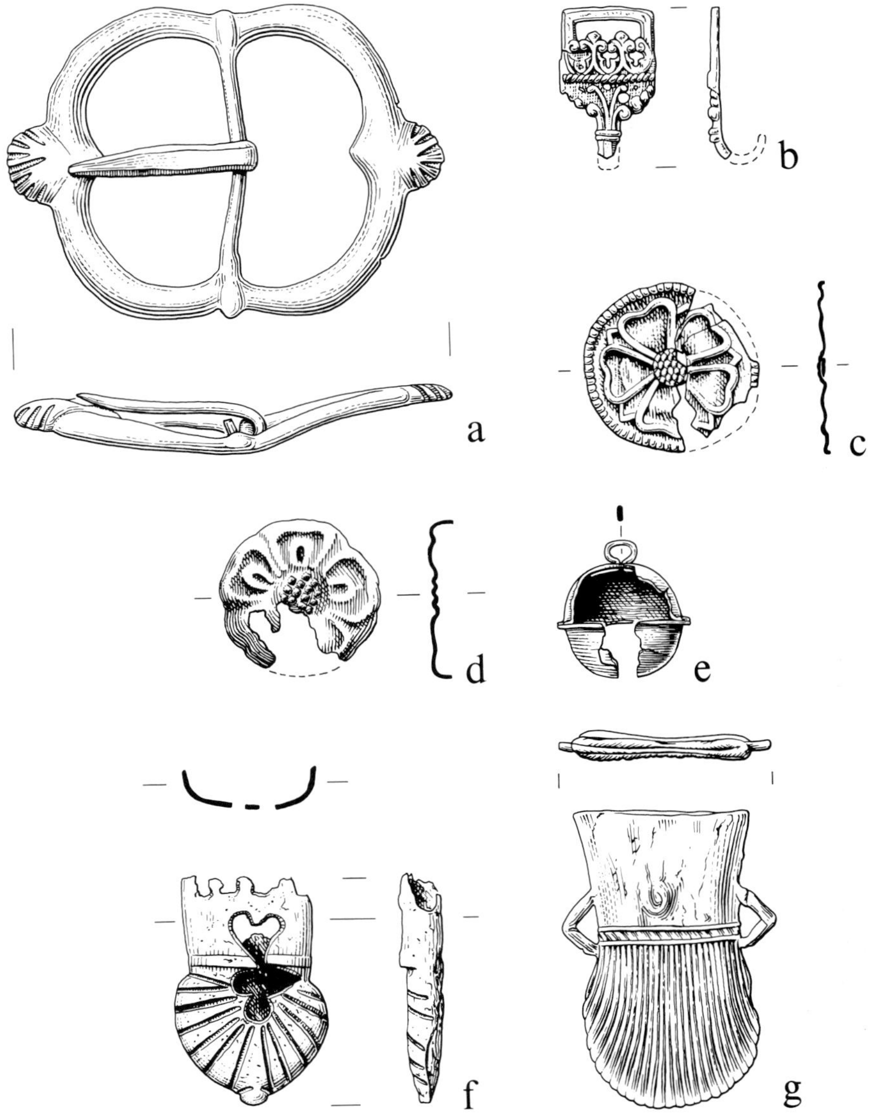

31. Ornaments of bronze and a pilgrim flask of lead: buckles (a, b), badges (c, d), and bell (e) from dog's collar or falcon's leg

in northern Spain (See p. 22 above). This was a favourite pilgrim destination though if the sea passage across the Bay of Biscay was undertaken it often had a penitential character which made the journey a memorable experience. A particularly interesting find was a pair of spurs; only the sides, neck and eight-pointed wheel-like rowel survive, but what gives both of these spurs an unusual character is that they were intended to be fitted with hinged side pieces to secure them to the wearer's boots. The spurs are not identical, but Mrs Blanche Ellis in her report draws attention to the fact that neither spur had been worn and both were apparently thrown away before the hinged pieces had been fitted. The use of such hinged pieces did not become common until the later 17th century so these spurs bear witness to an innovative design, perhaps not appreciated by the intended owners.

Richard III at Sandal

The usurpation by Richard duke of Gloucester in 1483 brought Sandal briefly into national prominence. While his brother Edward IV had moved easily throughout England, Richard had tended to build up his loyal following in the north. He had been brought up at Middleham in Wensleydale and had married Anne Neville of Middleham and Raby (**32**). He had spent money on Barnard Castle early in his reign and had founded a college of priests in Middleham church. However both Barnard Castle and Middleham were in remote valleys and Richard needed a secure base close to the main route between York and London. The choice fell upon Sandal (**25**). A series of orders survive in a royal signet letter book setting out the financial provision for a household and the ordinances or house rules by which it was to be organised. The annual maintenance allocation was to be 2000 marks (£1,344) supported from the rents of various manors throughout the north, including Raby, Barnard Castle, Skipton, Knaresborough, Pontefract and Tickhill, but involving support from as far west as Ulverston in Furness and as far east as Caistor in Lindsey. The household under the presidency of John de la Pole, earl of Lincoln, had a strict set of rules about worship, meal times, the supply of food and clothing, and the entertainment of strangers. Wages were to be strictly controlled by the treasurer; no extra serving boys were to be added to the household and no extra breakfasts were to be served other than to those on the payroll. This set of rules came into effect in July 1484.

However even in the first year of his reign Richard III was spending money on Sandal. The receiver of the manor of Wakefield, John Woderove, was ordered to spend money to "make a tower anew" and another item of expenditure refers to extensive repairs on a "small tower joined to the donjon". It is not clear whether both these payments concern the same tower. A later survey calls the Well Tower a "blockhouse" implying a strong tower capable of being held independently. This gives a clue to Richard's interest in Sandal. The Well Tower could be defended as a separate unit within the keep; the keep or donjon could be fortified in isolation from the rest of the castle. Even more significantly the whole castle could be held on its own, without Richard needing to be assured of the loyalty of the adjacent town. This factor distinguishes Sandal from York, Pontefract, Tickhill or Knaresborough, all of which were approached by a main entrance through a thriving town. A secretive and suspicious king would welcome this isolation in his main northern stronghold. Another factor in the choice of Sandal was filial piety. This was the spot where his father and namesake had died. The windows of the new tower looked over the battlefield of Wakefield past his father's memorial pillar to the scene of his brother Edmund's death on Wakefield bridge. Richard also maintained support for Towton chapel, consecrated where he and his brother had triumphed, and for Fotheringay church, where his father had subsequently been buried with honour.

As well as erecting a new tower to protect the well, John Woderove, the receiver of rents, was ordered in October 1484 to "cause a bakehouse and a

32. Richard III by John Rous flanked by his wife Anne and their son Edward

brewhouse to be builded within the castle of Sandal by the advice of the earl of Lincoln and others of the king's council living there". This new building would serve the household and garrison. New appointments were made in February 1485 of a constable, Richard Beeston, and a chaplain, Edmund Banke, perhaps indications of a king anxious about the loyalty of his followers in the north. There is a similar sequence of new building and new appointments at the two midland castles of Nottingham and Warwick, the former a strategic situation favoured by Edward IV, the latter chosen because of family ties and because of the crucial role it had played under Richard Neville "the kingmaker" in the previous thirty years. Richard's defeat at Bosworth in the summer of 1485 ended Yorkist rule at Sandal. The household was disbanded and no new works of similar scale were subsequently ordered. The castle's future role under the Tudors was far less central to the monarchy.

New building

The architectural evidence entirely supports the documentary record (**28**). The new works can be readily identified by the quality of their masonry and by the distinctive mix of their mortar. The main addition on the summit of the motte was the Well Tower or "New Tower" on the north side of the keep (**33**). It was a

33. Richard III's 'New Tower' (The Well Tower)

most ambitious structure, an irregular pentagon replacing the earlier semi-circular tower. It continued to protect the well which was over 40 metres (120 feet) deep. The basement was approached by a flight of fourteen steps from the ground floor of the donjon. Internally there was a privy and a fireplace. Externally there was a high quality of finish to the large rectangular blocks of ashlar facing-stone in the tower and its chimney stack though the latter has an awkward re-entrant angle. The tower rose through a further three storeys and may once have been as impressive as the Great Tower at Raglan. The use of hexagonal and octagonal towers was becoming increasingly common throughout the fifteenth century. This work at Sandal may have been envisaged as a first stage in re-casing all the circular towers in more fashionable and more defensible form while at the same time providing a better class of accommodation within. However excavation showed how hastily the work of re-casing had been done with a single thickness of facing stone on the perimeter wall and with the mortar slapped against the earlier circular tower; it is not surprising that this tower was in decay only eighty years later in 1562–4.

The second structure to be built was in the bailey north-west of the kitchen. The solid core and chamfered base, taken together with the octagonal plan, indicate that here was the base of the bakehouse chimney, perhaps with a side oven or vat as at Middleham. It is far less likely that this was the base of a tower protecting the west curtain wall, sally-port and keep ditch. As with the Well Tower on the keep it was grafted onto the existing wall as economically as possible. In the ditch near the curtain wall was situated an oven and this may be the last surviving part of the bakehouse which Richard III ordered to be built. It had a flue 2 metres long and led to a circular oven nearly a metre across; two stylobates or pad stones east of the flue may represent a shed to shelter those working there. This oven lay in the side of the ditch below the retaining wall which revetted the courtyard on its northern side and close to the archway leading to a sally-port. This back entrance had a rounded-headed arch of about 1480 made of well-carved sandstone. This entered a short passage in the thickness of the curtain wall. The outer entrance was subsequently blocked, probably in the Tudor period, and the passage was then used as a latrine for those working at the nearby oven (see **21**).

The third addition at this period were the abutments flanking the main gatehouse bridge where wing buttresses support what can have been little more than a theatrical gesture towards a military deterrent: the flanks were protected and the approach was commanded with a broader field of fire but it is not the massed defence seen sixty years earlier at Lancaster or contemporaneously at Kirby Muxloe in Leicestershire. It could be that this new work at Sandal represents an incomplete re-casing built in imitation of the south gate at Raglan (**34**).

The restriction of space in the bailey is emphasised by the two lengths of retaining wall: there is a long stretch north-south between the gatehouse and the barbican, and a shorter stretch running east-west from the west curtain wall towards the barbican ditch. These defined the edge of the bailey; they protected the crumbling Oaks rock from further decay, and they made possible the construction of additional lodgings for the steward close to the gatehouse and the enlarged bakehouse close to the kitchen. There were also changes in the area

34. Reconstruction of the castle in about 1560

south of the gatehouse where the Constable's Lodging was later to be built (**28**). Previously there had been a long shed (P) at right angles to the curtain wall and a stone built room (T) adjoining the Privy Chamber (W). At the time of Richard III's changes elsewhere in the castle there were modifications here which point to increases in the household. The shed (P) remained unaltered but it had a triangular walled garderobe (Q) added to its north side. The room (T) retained its overall dimensions but it had a small room (R) added to its north side; there was also a substantial stair base inserted in the south-east angle of this room and a less substantial division wall of lath and timber placed across the room. In the space between the east wall of Room T and the curtain wall two garderobes were constructed. The pottery groups in the filling of these two garderobes contained fragments of the same vessels, showing that they were in use simultaneously and served the same rooms. The filling of the garderobes needs to be considered within the overall pattern of the ceramic deposits.

Pottery and its uses

The pottery recovered in excavation from those four deposits which date to Richard III's reign total just over 2150 sherds. The majority came from the construction levels on the motte (965 sherds) and from the filling of the barbican ditch at level 2 (1034 sherds). Similarities between these two deposits are marked by parts of the same vessels being found in both locations. These were thick coarse sandy fabrics made in a variety of coloured surfaces and with a wide range of glazes. The normal vessel forms are jugs, cauldrons, cisterns and bowls. The jugs carry a wide range of decoration applied or incised on the shoulder of the pot; ring and dot ornament is common and one jug has a grotesque face. It is likely that these four pottery forms represent the normal domestic culinary vessels of the workmen on the site. The other very common pottery was the fabric known as late medieval gritty ware, produced at many kiln areas in west and south Yorkshire and occurring at Sandal in the forms of jugs, jars, cisterns, bowls and ladles. These vessels seldom carry much in the way of decoration except for a thumb-pressed strip around the neck. Three other distinctive fabrics are the jugs which are so hard fired in the kiln that they are close to stoneware in consistency, the jugs with a glossy green glaze often imitating high-class bronze vessel forms and the fine tableware in a white fabric and a glossy apple green glaze made in the Farnham region of Surrey; this last ware, known as "Tudor Green" because it is most often found on southern sites of the Tudor period, is found at Sandal in jugs, cups and a pottery whistle which may be a child's toy. Other deposits which can be dated to and associated with the new building work of Richard III's reign are found in the bakehouse, in the re-cut outer moat alongside the bridge abutments at the main entrance and in the infilled garderobe (NE) within the barbican tower (**54**).

The range of vessels shows the variety of domestic uses to which these items were put. The majority were required for cooking purposes and might be found wherever food storage and preparation took place. A few finer wares such as the "Tudor Green" jugs and cups were intended to be brought to the dining table or to the private chambers; these show where the serving of food and drink occurred. A large number of pottery vessels were found in the accumulation of soil in parts of the motte, especially in the north room, and these could indicate the rapid infill of unwanted areas with recently broken and immediately discarded material. Such material would have had a short period of use and be closely datable, unlike the pottery which was collected from various parts of the castle and deposited in the barbican ditch when the castle was brought back into service as a residence for the dukes of York in about 1450.

Changes in diet

The evidence provided by the pottery for zones of activity in the castle and for food consumption has to be set alongside the evidence provided by animal bone indicating preferences in diet. Nearly eight thousand fragments of bone were found dating from this short period of occupation during Richard III's work on the castle (**24**: Phase 2). Although bones of rabbit, chicken, goose and other fowl were found, attention centres upon the four main food animals. In order of importance these were cow (41.5%), sheep (23%), red and fallow deer (21%) and pig (14%). Horse made up 1% of the total. The only changes which these numbers represent on previous percentages are that cattle are continuing to rise in popularity and deer are continuing a steady decline from their greatest frequency in the 13th century. The low proportion of sheep (23%) instead of the normal level (29%) and the high proportion of pig (14%) instead of the normal level (8–9%) are isolated occurrences which may be explained by the special circumstances of the castle's occupation and the high standards of the household. There is unfortunately no indication of whether the castle kitchen relied on the produce of the manor or to what extent the kitchen steward had to rely on more distant markets. The few remains of cod and other sea fish show that for this commodity at least the inhabitants of Sandal castle had to look beyond their own immediate resources.

The presence of horse bones in this phase of occupation, as at most other times in the castle's use, is less an indication of the horse as a food animal but much more as a transport animal which was also used in hunting and warfare. Finds of horse shoes, bridle-bits, stirrups and harness buckles are all indications of the horse's importance even though few pieces of iron or of bronze bridle ornament date specifically to the reign of Richard III. The prevalence of hunting is shown by the loss of arrowheads though none are the distinctive bird bolt with a twin pronged end; presumably these would be lost in the park or in the river meadows. Rabbits and water birds might also be netted, while the depiction of the heraldic falcon with bells on its legs in the stained glass windows is another reminder of hunting for sport as well as for food. A bell of the type placed on falcons was found in the keep, dating from an earlier period of its occupation (**31e**; see p. 54). Such evidence is not conclusive since similar bells were placed on the collars of pet dogs or lap dogs. Deer would be chased by hounds until they were exhausted and then men on horseback could secure them in order to kill them for food. At all periods it is the light-weight fallow deer that predominate in the animal bone samples while the sturdier and speedier red deer is less common.

Labour and leisure

The evidence from the masonry buildings in Richard III's reign has already been discussed in parallel with the documentary references to Richard's construction

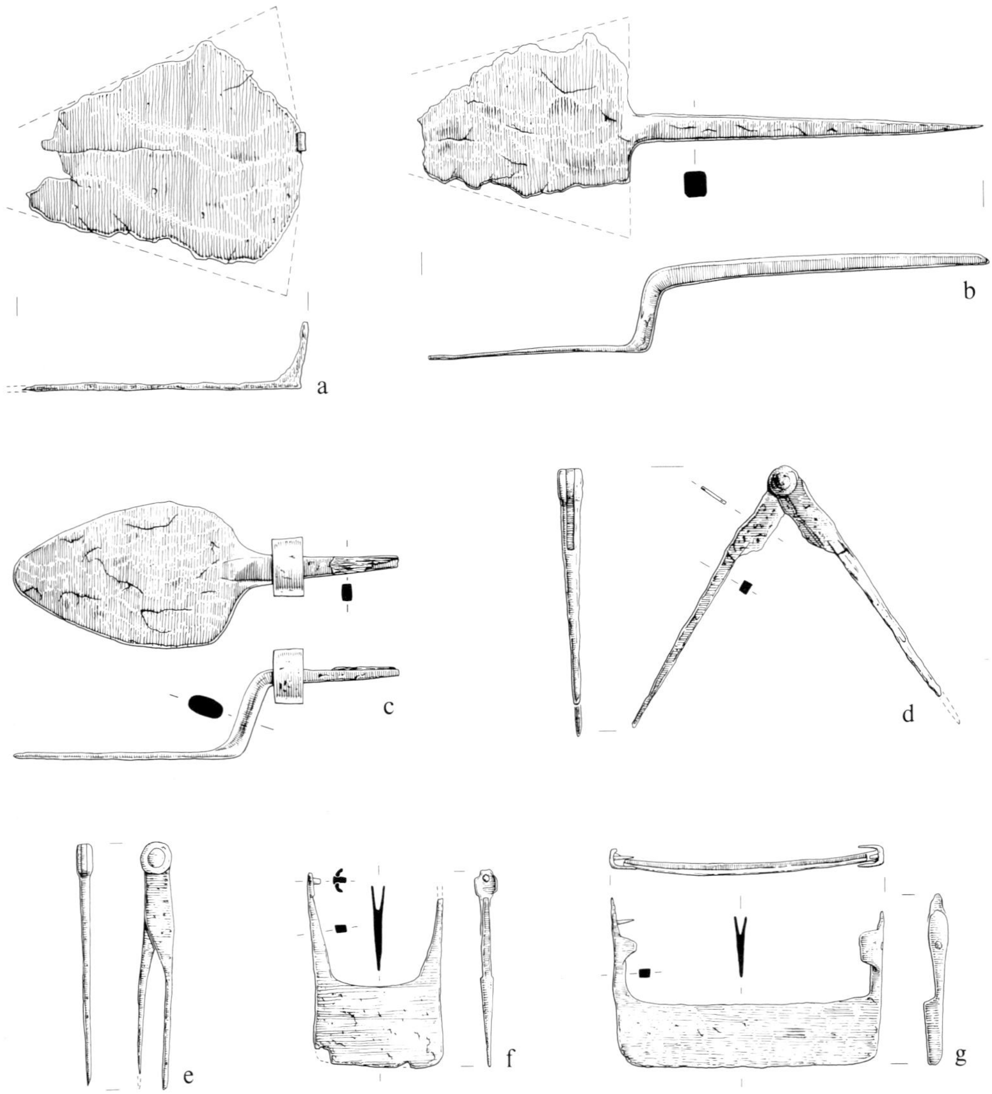

35. Building tools: trowels, compasses and spades

work. Further confirmation that building was in active progress is provided by discoveries of tools commonly used by builders. A trowel was found on the keep in the north room and another, with a rounded blade more appropriate for plastering, was discarded on the motte surface just outside the Well Tower (**35a,c**). Two pairs of compasses were discovered, one in the Great Chamber, the other in the courtyard near the Porter's Lodge (**35d,e**). Four spade irons were found in the Civil War forge or in the barbican ditch, but similar wooden spades, sheathed with iron to protect the blade from splitting, would be needed during the building process for mixing mortar or for digging the foundations of the Well Tower into the earth slopes of the motte (**35f,g**).

So far we have concentrated on the male and military aspects of the castle but the household also contained non-combatants such as a chaplain and a number of women. Evidence for the chaplain is scanty: apart from the pilgrims's flask of holy water (mentioned above p. 60) and the window glass depicting the Virgin Mary and the Infant Christ, there is nothing distinctively religious from the excavations. One must assume that there was a chapel or private oratory within the keep. It was possibly in tower 3 (the West Tower) near where the religious glass was found; it is here also that the 1562 drawing seems to show a turret or bell-cote rising beyond the Well Tower (**36**). The Tudor surveys make it clear that there was a chapel in the bailey: in 1538 its roof was in decay; in 1545–6 it was separately mentioned among those buildings that were in disrepair ("wholly prostrate"). It is not clear whether it was on an upper floor, perhaps over the larder and next to the kitchen. Another possibility is that it occupied the east-west aligned Building T near the gatehouse and adjacent to the well. Positive evidence for either suggestion is lacking.

The presence of women within the castle must be assumed, whether they came as noblewomen, wives of permanent officials, chamber-maids, kitchen wenches or washer-women. The evidence of dress items is ambiguous, though there was found a belt of silk decorated with pewter studs and with a heavy pewter buckle, and a silver strip with a delicate decoration of five-petalled flowers and foliage. Other items of textiles found at the castle, usually in the garderobe fills, included a silken ribbon woven through with a silver thread, pieces of linen, of felt and of plain weave wool. The occurrence of needles, thimbles and a bronze toilet implement (probably an ear scoop) is presumably an indication of feminine tasks, tastes and hygiene. However it is dangerous to jump to conclusions because the only ear-ring that was found occurred in a soldier's grave dating from the Civil War.

The interest of this brief episode of rebuilding and the installation of a royal household under Richard III lies in the close link between the documentary evidence and the archaeological evidence. The documents provide the names of the persons involved in the building work and in the conduct of the household. Archaeological investigation provides details of the speed with which that building construction was undertaken and of what animals the diet of the household was composed. This interaction of the sources and the wealth of supporting evidence is a major contribution towards a fuller understanding of the life style adopted by the Yorkist kings at Sandal.

Sandal and the Tudors

The death of Richard III on Bosworth Field in 1485 marked the end of Sandal Castle as a royal residence. During the next one hundred and sixty years the castle was fitfully kept in repair as a centre of local administration. It became a drain on royal revenue rather than a source of prestige. Under the Stuart kings it became an anachronism and was allowed to decay still further.

Many reasons lay behind this change of role. The foremost one was that the Tudor monarchs had no sentimental attachment to Sandal even though they kept the duchy of York lands together in name until 1558. Only the future kings Henry VIII and Charles I were briefly dukes of York but their elder brothers the princes Arthur (Tudor) and Henry (Stuart) died young; a separate duchy and household never really developed. Secondly the monarchs did not need these northern estates either for residential purposes or for dowries. Finally there was no question of granting away Yorkshire castles to favoured courtiers or of using these estates to endow newly created dukes and earls as happened with estates in Wales under Elizabeth. The Tudors were very wary of establishing a new aristocracy to replace those who had fallen in the Wars of the Roses or who had more recently been beheaded for treason. However throughout the reigns of the Tudors there was a very real danger of Scottish invasion. The Yorkshire castles might need to be refurbished against such an invasion, though only York and Scarborough were regularly kept in good repair.

All these factors contributed to the decline of Sandal. Its changed role meant that it normally housed a member of the local gentry as constable appointed to administer the extensive manor of Wakefield. It never needed to be held in readiness for a visit by the king and his court, though this might be the case at York (either at the castle and Grey Friars, or later at The King's Manor). Similarly it was never the venue for a regional legislative body as York was for the Council of the North. Even Sandal's role in local administration diminished when the Moot Hall was rebuilt in Henry VIII's reign and this became the normal place for holding the manor court once every three weeks. The records of that court were kept in the castle from 1560 to 1603, but were transferred to the new Moot Hall in the latter year. This event may well mark the end of a constable being permanently resident at Sandal Castle.

As a result of these changes the whole character of the castle altered. The keep and the barbican were needed only for the prison rooms which occupied their basements; there was no likelihood that the monarch or the dukes of York would visit and require housing here. The only purpose for which the defences were needed was the military threat of Scottish invasion. Essentially Sandal and the manor of Wakefield played a supporting role in the Tudor reigns. The revenue of the rents from the manor went to the repair of the defences at Berwick-on-Tweed between 1488 and 1522. At a later date (1566) Sandal was granted to Edward Carey who was captain of the garrison at Berwick and needed a residence midway between his military post and his family home in Essex. The need to keep Sandal in a state of defensive readiness was far less immediate than the task of maintaining Berwick in a well-provisioned and strongly fortified state.

The bailey buildings (**36**) were the hub of the castle. Originally there had been a circuit of interdependent buildings set against the outer wall. They had supported the necessary conduct of entertaining the dukes of York or Edward IV when he was in residence and had provided suitable lodgings for any visiting dignitaries on a northern tour of duty. There was an advantage in keeping the courtyard edge clear of buildings so that defence forces on the top of the barbican tower had an uninterrupted field of view to protect both barbican and keep. With the changed circumstances under the Tudors the major state rooms of hall and great chamber were allowed to fall into decay. Only two areas of the bailey had their buildings kept in good repair. At the south-west side the kitchen, larder, buttery, brewhouse and bakehouse were maintained to supply and serve the constable's household (**28**). The brewhouse and bakehouse had been substantially rebuilt under Richard III but the other buildings were nearly two centuries old. At the opposite end of the bailey close to the gatehouse a cluster of lodgings served the new function of the castle. Attached to the gatehouse was the Porter's Lodge either in the rooms over the gate passage or in a small half-timbered lodging on the right of the passage as one entered the castle. Beyond the gatehouse there were other half-timbered lodgings both to right and left. That on the right was the steward's residence with two storeys and at least three fireplaces. Far more impressive was the many gabled building on the left of the entrance. This was also of two storeys, perhaps with attics in the gables under the eaves. It had at least five fireplaces and elaborate roof finials. This was the Constable's Lodging and reflected that official's importance as the permanent functionary living in the castle, usually an aspiring member of a rising gentry family such as the Saviles of Thornhill or of Lupset or the Tempests of Tong. The administration of such an important manor gave many opportunities to wield power and exercise patronage. The holding of the manor courts, the appointment of court officials, the levying of fees and fines and the participation in commissions of enquiry all enhanced the constable's status and could be used to gain financial profit from the exercise of the post.

Another official attached to the castle was the chaplain of the oratory of St. Nicholas. Although these chaplains were regularly appointed until the suppression of the chantries in 1552 there is no evidence that they were permanently resident in the castle or that the chapel on the upper floor of the keep was regularly used. Instead they would act as household chaplains to the constable, thereby enhancing his importance, and might use as the chapel one of the little used or abandoned bailey buildings. The names of the chaplains are: 1486 Brian Balme alias Brian Milner; 1493 Matthew Shepherd; 1516 John Morice; 1545 Ralph Birkhead; 1553 Robert Burdhead (who may be the same man as Ralph). They received a small annual pension of £6 for their duties at the castle and they usually also served the chapel of St. Catherine in the parish church nearby.

There are three ways in which our knowledge of Sandal castle under the Tudors can be enlarged. The first is from the building surveys made on royal instructions to check upon the state of the fabric's repair; the second is from an ink and wash drawing that accompanied the survey of 1562; and the third is the evidence of the recent archaeological excavation. The three sources are complementary to one another but the drawing is the most informative and evocative. By contrast the archaeological record, being of a castle in disuse and decay, is less helpful than in the earlier periods of the castle's lively occupation.

Building surveys

Throughout the reign of Henry VII the main concern of the monarchy had been to secure peace at home and to prevent political interference from abroad. Little was spent on the royal works except near London and on the borders with Scotland. Accordingly the manorial revenues of Wakefield were diverted to support the defences and garrison of Berwick-on-Tweed and little else is known about Sandal castle in this reign. Henry VIII was anxious to maintain a high profile on the continent to rival the French king and to give support to the Papacy. The defence of Tournai and Calais was part of this policy; the lavish entertainment of The Field of the Cloth of Gold was diplomacy conducted on the grand scale. The overwhelming defeat of the Scots at Flodden in 1515 lifted the threat on the northern border until near the very end of his reign. However the religious problems brought about by the king's divorce of Catherine of Aragon hastened the need for coastal defence along the southern and eastern shores. This in turn led to the requirement of money to pay for these defences from 1535 onwards. The suppression of the lesser monasteries in 1536 prompted a popular revolt, The Pilgrimage of Grace, in which the Yorkshire abbots were implicated and some conservatively-minded gentry were closely involved. It was necessary for Henry to learn about the state of repair in which his northern castles were. To achieve this a survey was ordered in 1538; this is in two parts, firstly a circuit of the castle to indicate where repair work was needed, and secondly a summary of each type of material and the quantities required. In the keep (or "high tower") a number of floors were decayed or unsafe and the roof leads needed repair; in the Well Tower or "new tower" there were stone corbels and wooden boards missing. At the entrance to the keep the wooden floor of the room over the portcullis was decayed. Moving on to the barbican tower the surveyors found that it too had its floors and roofs in decay. The two bridges linking the barbican to the keep and to the courtyard were both in decay. Within the bailey buildings there is a similar tale of decay affecting the floors, walls and roofs. This afflicted the lodgings adjoining the kitchen, the great hall, the lesser hall (elsewhere called the great chamber), the chapel and the new lodgings wing. The kitchen chimneys were in decay as was the timber bridge outside the main gate. Two points to note here are that the "new lodging" for the constable had a chamber floor in decay even though it was only sixty years old and the other is that the chapel is listed as if it were a separate building in the bailey replacing the room in the keep. The only areas which get good reports are the bakehouse and brewhouse even though that did not have a horse driven mill or any horses to work it. The castle well was in good repair though one other well had been stopped or closed down. Presumably it was the well in the bailey near the gatehouse which was in use and the well in

Richard III's tower on the keep that had been closed or sealed off. In terms of defence the castle possessed only two iron guns though it also had 70 staves, perhaps for pike heads or halberds. The amount of material needed to effect the repairs was estimated as a ton of iron, a ton of timber for beams, 10,000 feet of timber planks, fifty fothers of lead (975 cwt.) for roofing and also masons' work to the value of £66 (some £15,000 at present day prices). It is not known to what extent this report was acted upon, though one might expect that serious attention would be given to all the bridges and to the constable's lodgings. The surveyors may have painted a blacker picture in order to cover themselves against any accusations of inefficiency or neglect of duty.

Towards the end of Henry VIII's reign fears of a French invasion were strong, perhaps in conjunction with a Scottish pincer movement. The defences of Carlisle and Berwick were strengthened, a new castle was proposed at Wark or at Norham on the Tweed and a citadel and defence line was built at Hull to protect the approach up the Humber. In 1545 a further survey was made of Sandal. The visitors spoke favourably of its situation, just as the antiquary John Leland had on his tour some ten years earlier. Expressed in modern spelling their report was:

> "The said castle stands very fair and stately, one little mile distant from the town of Wakefield. It is strongly defended with a fair wall seven feet thick, and is situated upon a rocky hill surrounded by a deep and broad dry ditch. The towers [within the keep] are five in number standing close together on the west part of the castle, of which three are in a convenient state of repair covered over with lead and with the timber work of the roof beginning to decay; the lead of one of them being already removed and the others standing untiled. The gate and entry is likewise roughly built which together with the walls are in a good state except that one small part of the wall of the forechamber [barbican] is fallen down; the necessary repairs will cost the king's majesty ten pounds or thereabouts. The principal buildings [in the bailey] are hall, chambers, chapel, and service rooms; these are wholly prostrate except for the kitchen which is fair and large. If an expenditure of 53s. 4d. is made in timber, tiling and slating they may still be kept standing.
>
> The steward's and constable's lodging being divided from the rest are of timber and plasterwork. They are suitable to be maintained as they serve not only for the steward for the time being but also for the Keeper of the Park. It will be necessary to spend £100 in tiling, slating and plastering the said places where they are decayed."

Again it is uncertain how much was done in the way of repairs, though since the constable continued to occupy his lodgings it is likely that this building and the kitchen were fully maintained. Reference to removal of lead from the keep roof is confirmed by an Exchequer court case in which John Peck of Wakefield had been tried for removing lead and stone from the castle. This accusation was brought by Sir Richard Tempest who was an opponent of the constable Sir Henry Savile. Peck was one of Savile's tenants. This court case may be part of the political rivalry between these two local families.

Under Edward VI and Mary there is no record of any inspection of Sandal or of any other Duchy of York castles. However under Elizabeth there is a regular process of inspection ordered by the Privy Council as part of a systematic attempt to keep tight control upon Crown expenditure. The constable was Sir John

Tempest and his task was to supervise the manor courts and the collection of the crown's rents. Prisoners from the manor's townships were imprisoned in the basements of Sandal's towers. As had happened under Henry VIII there were surveys made. The first of these was in 1562. It reported that Sandal castle "was especially to be maintained because it stands in a strong country of men, amongst whom if any rebellion should happen (which God forbid) this castle must be the defence against it". The two dangers were a revival of religious conservatism in favour of Roman Catholicism fermented by secret Jesuit teaching and the invasion by Scottish armies in favour of Mary Queen of Scots as ruler of England. These twin perils did not subside until the execution of Mary (at the Yorkist castle of Fotheringay) in 1587 and the defeat of the Spanish Armada in 1588.

When the survey of northern castles was prepared in 1562 by Sir Ambrose Cave he took with him an unknown artist to make drawings or "plotts" of the buildings. Drawings of eight castles still survive in the Public Record Office in London, including Knaresborough, Pontefract and Conisbrough. The evidence provided by the drawing of Sandal (**36**) will be considered later in this chapter, but these drawings should be seen as an aide-memoire to assist the Privy Council to visualise the castle which they were discussing and the problems that the surveyors had noted.

Two years later in 1564 another commission of enquiry was appointed; a jury of twelve men under the leadership of Hugh Savile was empanelled; they visited the castle and reported their findings. Again there is a sharp contrast in the conditions between the inhabited parts which are still in tolerable repair (the porter's lodge, the constable's lodging and the kitchen) and the other courtyard buildings, the barbican and the keep where roofs, floors and sometimes the walls themselves were in decay. However where rooms in the keep and the barbican were in use as prisons with floors of stone or rock, then those parts were reported as in good repair. As far as the responsibility for the repairs was concerned the jury reported "when and by whom these buildings decayed we do not know but daily they do decay". As to the future the jury considered that "the whole castle of Sandal ought to be repaired because there is no other stronghold nearby adjoining to the same and £500 would repair it well and sufficiently".

A third report was ordered in December 1565 from Sir Thomas Gargrave and Christopher Mather. They returned their findings in January 1566. This was the third occasion that the castle had been visited in January, when the weather was likely to be inclement and the faults to the roofs would be most obvious. The catalogue of faults, cracked walls, decayed timberwork, "putrified" roofs and unsafe rooms is much as before, though this time the actual dimensions of the buildings are given. The rooms still in good repair are the gatehouse with Porter's Lodge adjoining, the Constable's Lodging (in fairly good repair) and the Kitchen. The outermost walls of the castle were broken in four places and would cost about £50 to repair. However whereas the previous reports had given general comments about the need for repair Gargrave and Mather made quite specific proposals. They considered that there was enough hewn stone and rubble stone to make the necessary masonry repairs and if that did prove to be insufficient then the manor possessed a stone quarry close to the castle. They considered that there was sufficient timber of all kinds within the park of Sandal and within the outwoods of Wakefield within a distance of two miles from the castle. Their most drastic solution concerned the lead roofs. All the expanses of lead had been recorded, being specially underlined in the report and further totalled in the margin. The commissioners' recommendation was that all the lead should be sold; all the roofs at that time covered with lead should be replaced by new roofs of steeper pitch and covered with slate stones which were in abundant supply in the district. The sale of the lead would pay for all or the greater part of the repairs. Gargrave and Mather reported that this would make the castle "both a house of defence in time of need against commotions or strife and a lodging convenient for any nobleman resident there to secure the peace of the countryside". Three or four hundred pounds well laid out would bring the castle into a good state of repair and of suitable strength to support the government. It was therefore urged that the castle should be repaired and maintained.

Queen Elizabeth acted swiftly upon this report and appointed "a nobleman" to live there. Edward Carey, the son of her cousin Lord Hunsdon, was granted the lease of the castle late in 1566 with the requirement of keeping it in good repair. He took up residence on occasion and in 1569 he supplied men and arms to support the queen when the disturbance known as The Rebellion of the Earls broke out in the northern counties. Sandal castle was fulfilling exactly the role Sir Thomas Gargrave had envisaged for it.

Carey continued to use Sandal while he was acting as governor at Berwick-on-Tweed but in 1586 he conveyed the castle to his son-in-law Sir John Savile of Howley. Two years later Savile was appointed constable, porter, steward and park paler (or keeper). These were mainly honorific titles. However the parks were an important perquisite of the castle, and will need to be examined in relation to diet later in this chapter. The castle was still giving cause for concern. An enquiry in 1592 was prompted by the rumour that Sandal along with the royal castles of Tickhill and Pontefract was "in great ruin and decay" and that the lead and timber had been purloined by ill-intentioned persons. Again it was suggested that stone slates should replace any lead roofs; the danger of theft still faces many parochial church councils with vulnerable medieval churches. The 1592 report finding was that "the residence of this castle is near ruinous and in great decay". Indeed there is no evidence that Sir John Savile ever lived in the castle and the same is true for his successor as constable, Sir Thomas Savile, appointed in 1619. A further Privy Council report in 1610–11 is equally pessimistic. It seems likely that the building of the new Moot Hall in Wakefield with its capacity for holding the court records and for providing prisons for offenders ensured that Sandal castle lost its need to be kept in good repair. The religious differences were no longer a serious problem despite the Gunpowder Plot and with the accession of James VI of Scotland to the throne of England the northern border was secure from any major invasion threat.

An Elizabethan drawing

The historical records, therefore, paint a picture of government concern but of increasing decay. However an even better picture (**36**) is provided by the draughtsman who accompanied Sir Ambrose Cave on his tour of inspection in the spring of 1562. He gives the only authentic depiction of the medieval castle, as he did of the other Duchy of Lancaster castles, such as Clitheroe, Knaresborough, Pontefract and Tickhill. Discounting the disproportionate oak trees which suggest the luxuriance of Sandal Park around the castle this picture shows all the buildings mentioned in the surveys. The artist tends to accentuate the height of buildings at the expense of the breadth and his perspective is sometimes at fault. He also combines information from two separate viewpoints in order to show the entire castle. He first used as his platform the gatehouse or the turret just north of it on the curtain wall so that he could draw the bailey buildings; then he moved outside the gatehouse onto the outer bank in order to draw the keep, curtain wall and the gatehouse.

By choosing two separate viewpoints he was able to illustrate all the important aspects of the survey. He also marked the point between the two main gate towers on the keep where the wall was "cloven" with the stones pulled apart as the crack had developed; he indicated the area of fallen wall near the Constable's Lodging where the battlemented parapet had been replaced by timber rails. The other faults on the curtain walls were not visible on this drawing.

This illustration gives a good impression of a castle with its main buildings erected in the thirteenth century. The keep is shown with its disproportionate arrow slits, the twin-towered fore-building and the arcaded entrance passage. To the left of it lies the barbican, again with long arrow slits and an upper window with a shouldered "Caernarvon" head. Between the keep and the barbican is shown the kitchen, beyond them within the bailey, with a roof of stone tiles and a many-gabled smoke louvre; the massive chimney belongs to the new bakehouse and a grey wash on the drawing may indicate a plastered or a smoke-stained wall surface. The state buildings of Great Hall, Great Chamber and the lodging with its ornate circular turret are vigorously drawn; many of their details have been confirmed by excavation. In all the buildings so far mentioned it is the details of their upper floors, windows, roofs and chimneys that are given by the Elizabe-

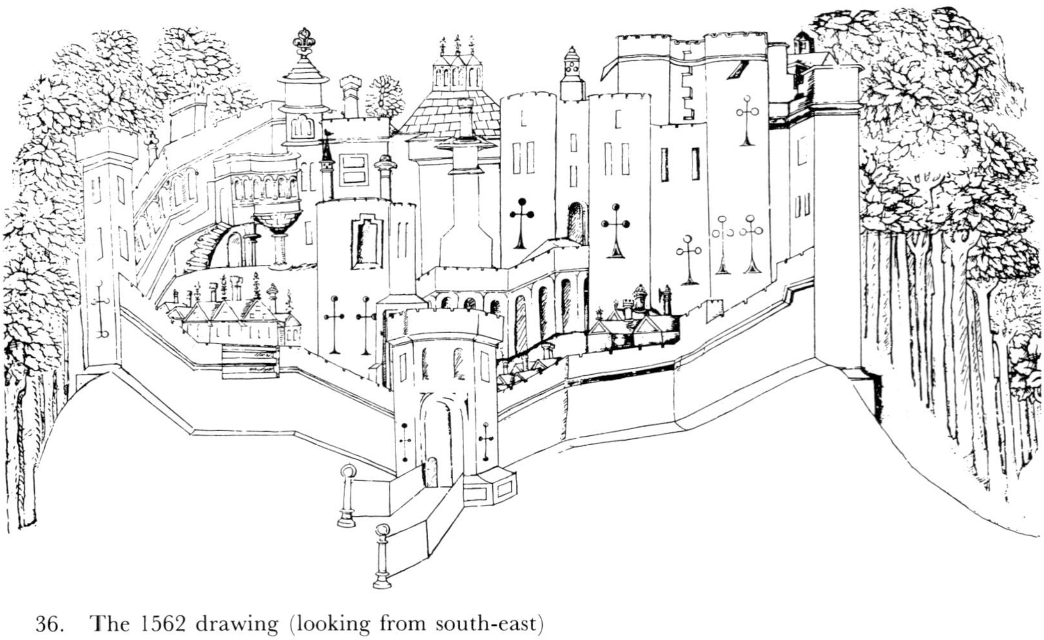

36. The 1562 drawing (looking from south-east)

than drawing which so valuably augment the information of their ground plans provided by excavation. However for the gatehouse and for the half-timbered lodgings blocks archaeological work has been able to show little; without the 1562 drawing any reconstruction would be impossible. The lodgings were timber framed with plastered wall surfaces and with slate or tiled roofs. The gable ends had elaborate finials and the chimney pots were castellated or were circular with pierced conical caps. The insubstantial foundations make it difficult to offer any positive information about them, but the pottery evidence strongly suggests that these timber buildings were erected in the period 1475–1525 and that occupation finished during the sixteenth century. Timber buildings were not necessarily lacking in prestige. The many-gabled lodging block erected at Nottingham Castle for Edward IV and Richard III was entirely timber-framed towards the courtyard, while the Horseshoe Cloister of 1478–81 at Windsor Castle is of similar construction. Even later in date is the President's Lodging at Queens College, Cambridge. What was appropriate for the head of a Cambridge college with royal links was equally appropriate for the constable and permanent officials of a royal castle in Yorkshire.

The gatehouse stands in the foreground of the drawing. Although the foundations and stepped plinth still survive, nothing else stands above the footings. The drawing shows clearly the simpler round-headed windows and arch of the earlier central work and the arrow-slits converted to gun ports. The rectangular upper windows belong to the later buttressing which is almost theatrical in its composition and could be easily outflanked. Stone balls from the gate passage outer bridge (or from a similar bridge in the bailey over the barbican ditch) were recovered in the excavation. It is not clear whether they were purely an architectural embellishment or whether they had later been used as ammunition in the Civil War siege.

The archaeological evidence

It is now necessary to consider the archaeological evidence to see how far it confirms the impressions provided by the documents and the drawing and to see in what directions it is capable of giving new insights into those areas of study not mentioned in the documents. In general the thrust of the material evidence is concerned with the living conditions and the diet of the occupants. It is clear that occupation concentrated in the lodgings blocks either side of the gatehouse. It was here that the pottery was most frequently found, with nearly 5,000 sherds deposited in that part of the barbican ditch closest to this area. There were only slight traces of a building south-west of the gatehouse: a garderobe and the retaining wall running along the inner edge of the barbican ditch presumably also served the porter's lodge and/or the steward's lodge in this entrance area. Similarly the sequence in the Constable's Lodging (PRT) suggests that three or possibly four buildings backed up against the curtain wall with their gable ends facing into the courtyard. Door and window mouldings in stone and part of a plaster cornice from these lodgings was found in excavation. The most substantial room (T) was set on stone foundations and had two garderobes in the space between its end wall and the curtain wall. A second room (R) was newly built in this phase of the castle's occupation; it had an oven in its front wall and a well-constructed fireplace flanked by two small circular bake-ovens in its back wall which was formed by the medieval curtain wall. Within the room (T) was a garderobe which went out of use in this period. In the courtyard in front of this room was the bailey well which was only filled in at the very end of the castle's occupation so must have continued in use throughout the 16th century. A third room (P) was of timber-framed construction on a low sill wall. It also had a flagstone hearth set against the curtain wall. North of this room was a triangular garderobe Q which was also in use at this phase. This may have been accessible from the courtyard but it is possible that for privacy the garderobe was incorporated within another room of which all trace has been removed by site erosion. The garderobe Q was filled with rubbish in the late sixteenth century. The pollen grains in this and the other garderobes showed evidence of weeds growing nearby, particularly dandelion and daisy. This probably indicates such weeds growing in the courtyard, on the wall tops and lodged in the gutters, all pointing to neglect on building maintenance. There was no clear evidence of structural alteration in the kitchen during the Tudor period but pottery found within it and in the adjacent bakehouse was identical to that dumped in the upper layer of the barbican ditch. The quantities of pottery on the keep and the barbican were extremely small, being confined to one Cistercian-ware cup from the north room on the keep and a group of three industrial vessels outside the Well Tower. All this evidence points to a contraction of the use of the castle in Tudor times.

Pottery and metalwork

The pottery of this period totalled nearly 5,000 sherds representing about 600 different vessels deposited with rubbish in the barbican ditch and another 325 sherds representing about 100 vessels from the six garderobes in use situated in the lodgings near the gatehouse. The range of pottery varied from the local wares of the Yorkshire kilns using the gritty ware traditions of the Pennines through to the local fine tablewares which copied the Dutch redwares and the white fabric green-glazed "Tudor Green" of Surrey. These glazed wares came in a variety of forms: jugs, bowls, dishes, ladles, saucepans and chafing dishes (dish warmers). There were also distinctive vessels imported from abroad: tall glazed jars known as "albarellos" from Malaga in Spain, flat circular flasks from Martincamp in northern France and a wide variety of brown or grey stoneware jugs from the Rhineland kilns of Raeren, Frechen and Cologne.

This period witnessed a change from medieval forms to the modern pottery forms of chalice, cup, bowl and dish treated with a high gloss overall finish in yellow or black glaze. The yellow wares are normally associated with the Midlands but may well have been made in Yorkshire. The black wares (**37**) are often known as Cistercian wares since they were first found at Kirkstall abbey in 1893 and it was thought that the monks had made them there. However it is now known that Potovens near Wakefield was a principal place of local manufacture by potters using the natural resources of the Outwoods. A quite distinctive form of decoration was the applied disc of creamy white clay formed into rosettes, flowers, face-masks and a stag. Other products of these kilns were chalice-like drinking cups, candlesticks, cup-shaped table salt cruets and little figurines intended for table or sideboard decorations. The yellow ware forms include chamber-pots, chafing dishes, cylindrical bowls and a four-lobed cruet. There is a

37. Typical group of Cistercian ware
showing three two-handled cups, a candlestick (*centre right:* top broken), tall beaker (*centre left*) and a jug (*left*), from Sandal and Potovens

distinct break in style between the Cistercian wares and yellow wares of the 16th century found at Sandal and those of the Civil War siege period suggesting a forty-year break in occupation. The lack of Metropolitan type slipwares and of the vessel form of "tyg" or mug tends to confirm this gap in the use of the castle.

While the pottery throws light on cooking and eating habits, the vessel glass illustrates toilet and domestic habits. The glass from the seven garderobes in and near the Constable's Lodging includes blue body and clear green glass of fine quality as well as the more typical opaque green glass from the forest glasshouses; the existence of such glasshouses is likely in west Yorkshire but has not yet been proved. In the bed chambers of the lodgings there would be glass urinals to cater for the nobleman's comfort during the night and for his servant to check the urine for ailments or disease on the following morning. The urine might either be poured down the garderobe pit or be kept for sale to fullers as a cleansing agent in the preparation and dying of cloth. Also in the bedchamber would be hand-washing bottles or "ewers" and glass bowls or "lavers"; there would be glass drinking cups and probably wine storage jars or "cisterns" and pouring jugs. In the highest quality households some of these items would be of bronze or of precious metal; in the medium quality household these would be of glass or pottery and the evidence from Sandal is of this nature. However parts of bronze cauldrons and plates were found in the Constable's Lodging and in the well in the courtyard. A different activity is shown by glass vessels in the drawbridge pit of the gatehouse and in the adjacent part of the barbican ditch. A glass distillation vessel and three pottery bowls suggest that the room over the gatehouse was used for the practice of alchemy, but it is not known what the end product was intended to be.

There was little among the metal finds that was informative or distinctive. Two decorated lead weights may be connected with the practice of alchemy, but could equally well be connected with a pair of scales in the larder. A foliage finial in bronze almost certainly came from a decorative knife handle. Scissors from the Constable's Lodging and thimbles from adjacent garderobes or ditches indicate dressmaking or household stitchery. An axe-head in the Great Hall and a pair of compasses (**35e**) in the Porter's Lodge may represent building activity in this period. The defence of the castle is modestly represented by a dagger-guard or cross piece made of bone and an iron spearhead ready to be mounted on a wooden staff (as mentioned in the 1538 Survey). Two stone bowls or mortars were abandoned in the blocked sally-port where it looked as if they had been used as chamber-pots. Outside the Constable's Lodging there was furnace slag and a furnace lining indicating minor metal working, probably in connection with the fitting out of the Constable's Lodging. The raw material of iron seams occurred locally and the preliminary working was done in the parks and the outwoods, judging by the evidence contained in the Manor Court Rolls of nuisances there committed. The modest character of the Tudor period occupation is marked by the loss of only four Tudor coins, all in soil that was deposited or accumulated at the Civil War. By contrast in those levels of building occupation and of barbican ditch fill attributable to the Tudor phase the coin losses were of the preceding half-century: a groat of Henry VI and two French jettons of 15th-century date.

Food remains

Evidence of diet was provided by the animal bone discarded in the garderobes and in the barbican ditch. There was a large quantity of bone recovered in the excavation; over 1400 major bones of the six main types of large mammal were found (**24**: Phase 1). This is twice as much as in any other phase of the castle's occupation and eight times as much as in any other half-century; this suggests a greater readiness to dump waste material in privies, ditches, pits or any other convenient hole when it fell into disuse. The proportions represented in the six species are cattle: 41.5%, sheep: 28.5%, fallow deer: 19%, pig: 9%, horse: 1.5% and red deer: 0.5%. There had been a steady increase in the proportions of cattle and sheep since 1300. This suggests that there had been a gradual clearance of pasture fields and meadows in the Calder valley for cattle grazing and a similar extension of arable fields where sheep could graze on the fallow and the stubble after harvest. This is supported by the evidence of pollen analysis with high proportions of cereals, grasses and the weeds of cornfields and cleared grazing land. By contrast the pig was in decline as a food animal supplied to the castle. This may show that the pig was increasingly excluded from the managed woodlands and parks, and also that the wild pig as an animal of the chase was no longer to be found near Wakefield.

The parks

The proportion of fallow deer was also declining steadily though it still represented the third most usual food source. However it is clear that fallow deer kept within the park fence or "pale" were an important ingredient in the food supply. They would certainly have been a perquisite that made the post of Constable an attractive duty for local gentry especially when combined with the honorary title of Park Keeper and Paler. The use of the park was rented out and woodwards would be employed to maintain the fences and clear the undergrowth. Two of the surveys (1545, 1564) mention the park and its deer. That of 1564 is the fuller survey and shows that there were three parks stocked with deer (**38**). The park around the castle was of about 32 acres and contained

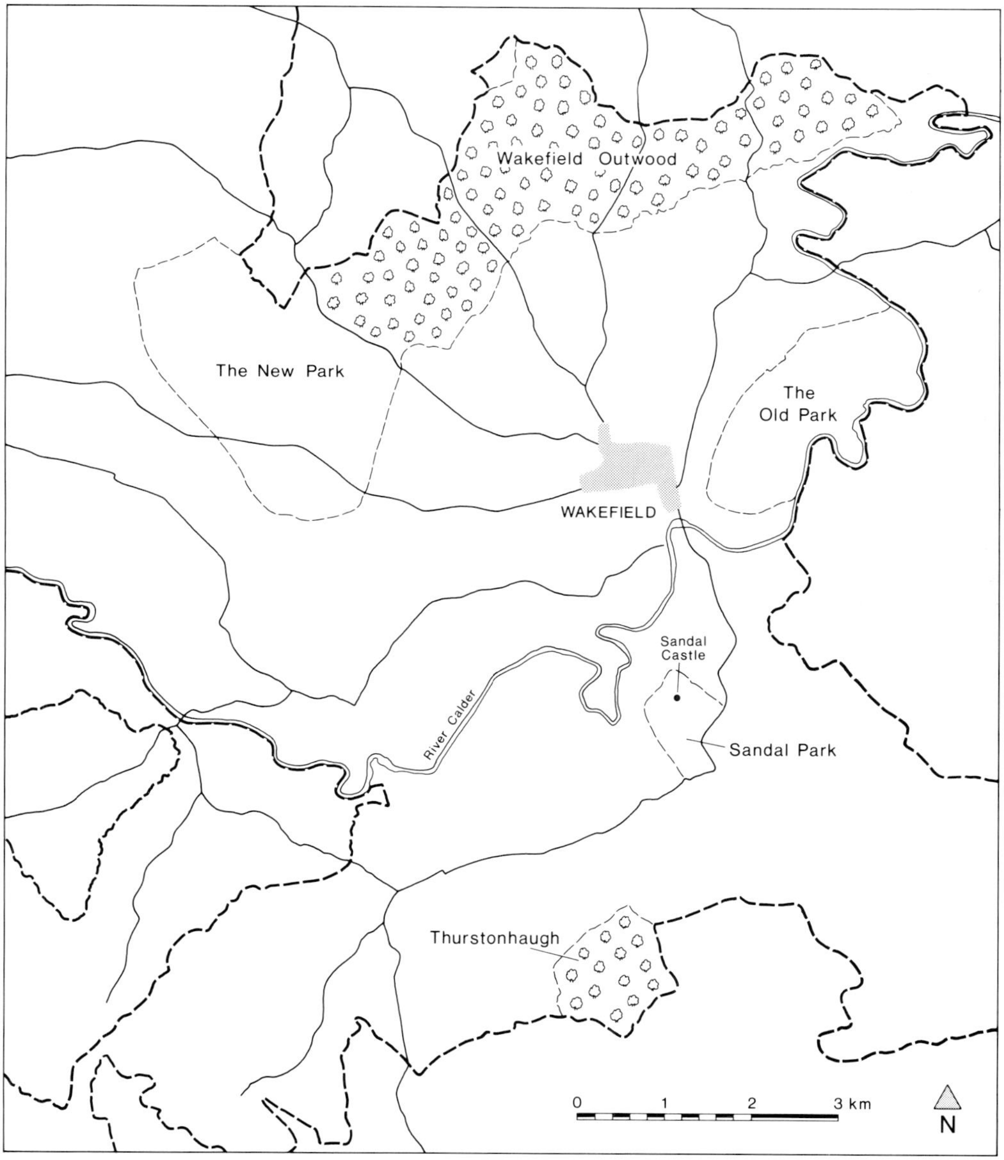

38. Map of the parks and woods around Sandal

20 deer; the same acreage is recorded in 1304 but it was estimated at 40 acres in 1545. The second park, The Old Park, east of Wakefield in Stanley township, was nearer 100 acres and contained 30 deer. The feeding or "herbage" in the park was sufficient, the park fences or pales were in good repair, but only one of the three lodges was well maintained. This fact suggests that after Sandal ceased to be a royal residence hunting as a sport had declined and that the deer were culled for their venison by shooting or netting. The New Park was mainly in Ossett township west of Wakefield and occurs as early as 1297; it was much larger than the Old Park and in 1564 was stocked with 300 deer, though this number may be double the normal stock because of winter feeding. It is normally estimated that a park of 100 acres should support 20 deer. The fences and lodges were all in good order, and some parts of the boundary bank and ditch can still be traced today.

The red deer formed a small part of the diet. They may have been kept on the three parks near Wakefield. It is more likely that they were caught in the wilder ground at Erringden Park (**3**) near Sowerby or that they roamed freely over the Pennine uplands and were hunted with horse and hounds. In the woodland of the parks and the Wakefield outwoods another source of food would be the game birds of pheasant, partridge, woodcock and snipe, but medieval wildfowlers took any bird they could net, trap or shoot. The bird bone at Sandal in the Tudor period includes domestic chicken and goose together with a variety of wildfowl.

The fish diet included cod, presumably traded from east coast ports, and carp which must have been netted in specially dug ponds or "stews". One such stew lay in the park close to the castle, another at the mill below the castle where Milnthorpe is the suggestive place name, and a third lay within the Old Park in Stanley, possibly using an abandoned river loop. River fish, none of which were identified at Sandal castle in the bone material, were caught in the Calder at specially constructed fish weirs where nets or wicker baskets could be placed in the gap alongside the stone-built weir. All the shell fish (oyster, cockle and a few mussel) indicated a regular though small supply shipped from Grimsby to provide oysters from the Wash and cockles from the Humber estuary. During this period the religious Reformation meant that the insistence on Friday and Lent fasting weakened. The necessity to catch and eat fish was no longer a firm obligation but instead became a desirable supplement to the diet.

In some senses the Tudor period is the most rewarding era in the castle's history. There is a regular and interesting documentary record. There is the attractive drawing of the castle as it was at the start of Elizabeth's reign. Furthermore there is an agreeably close coincidence between the historical and the archaeological evidence. Yet in another sense it is a disappointing period. The documents show a castle in decay, reduced to a care and maintenance basis, not exactly in mothballs but with occupation restricted to a limited group of buildings and used for a narrow range of purposes. The drawing was commissioned in order to show the cracks and the masonry faults. The archaeological material shows a far lower standard of cleanliness and household provision. The great days of Sandal had passed, as they had for Pontefract and Conisbrough. There was to be no earl of Calderdale making Sandal his mansion house, unlike the Cliffords, earls of Cumberland, at Skipton or the Cavendishes, earls of Devonshire, at Bolsover. The Elizabethan age saw new houses built at Heath,

Barlborough and New Hall in Pontefract on fresh sites and with light, airy and spaciously planned structures. Sandal was a creation of the barons from the middle ages. It was used as a stepping-stone by the upwardly mobile minor gentry of the locality; it was spurned by the brilliant courtiers of the Tudor renaissance.

The Civil War

At the outbreak of the Civil War in 1642 Sandal castle was ill prepared to play a decisive role on either side. That it figured at all in the hostilities was due to the determination of the local Royalists to make a stand for king and country. Although the war often divided families and brought conflicting loyalties, it is a fair generalisation to say that most of the nobility and country gentry supported king Charles I and his view of the divine right of kings to act according to their religion and their conscience. Equally it is fair to say that most of the townsfolk, the yeoman farmers and the merchants supported Parliament because of the heavy and arbitrary taxation that Charles had levied. The church was split with the High Church faction favouring the supreme authority of the kings and the bishops and with the low church faction preferring a greater freedom in matters of belief and acknowledging that there was room for differing forms of worship.

The early course of the war had been fought between the Parliamentarians, who held London and the south-eastern counties of England, and the Royalists with their main support in the north and the west, who attempted to launch a combined movement and so sweep down to London through the undeclared midland counties. At first the superiority of the Cavalier horsemen dashingly led by Prince Rupert seemed likely to win the war for the king. Many of the Royalists had seen military service on the continent during the Thirty Years War; they were better trained and better equipped than the forces of Parliament. The crushing victory of Edgehill (1642) near Banbury suggested an early end to the war in the king's favour. However the ports of Hull and Gloucester held out for Parliament and gave Cromwell time to raise and train an army in the eastern counties. This army was successful at the battle of Marston Moor, fought near York in July 1644 as Prince Rupert tried to lift the Parliamentary siege of that city. Cromwell's cavalry charges proved to be the decisive factor. The Parliamentary army under Fairfax and Cromwell undertook stricter training and became a better disciplined force than the Royalists. After Marston Moor the Parliamentary forces never lost a full-scale battle. In June 1645 at Naseby in Northamptonshire the crucial battle of the first Civil War was won by the army of Parliament. Then it became a matter of containing and mopping up the isolated Royalist resistance. Although there were occasional victories in cavalry skirmishes the Royalist cause was reduced to defending individual towns, isolated castles and resolute country houses. These held out as long as their commanders entertained serious hopes of relief; these positions were more of a nuisance value, particularly to the non-combatant towns and villages whose stores and crops they raided. Some towns, such as Colchester and Newark-on-Trent, resisted for two or three years and needed to be surrounded by siege lines specially dug to prevent escape or relief. Usually the town garrison depended on a strong, well-provisioned castle as its main base. Other isolated castles were starved or bombarded into submission. This is what happened at Sandal.

Deaths at the castle

Major Thomas Beaumont of Whitley had garrisoned Sandal Castle for the king and placed a Major Ward in command of a small contingent. However Ward did not enjoy his command for many months because it is reported that he fell while descending some steps in the castle and broke his neck. One skeleton (**39**) found among the nine burials in the bailey may well be Major Ward. He was buried in a coffin and had suffered from a fractured skull and consequent haemorrhage. There were no other injuries apparent on the skeleton.

Major Ward was replaced by Colonel George Bonivant, the garrison was strengthened and hostilities around Sandal were pursued more actively in 1645. Early in that year Sir Thomas Fairfax entrusted the siege of Sandal to Sir John Savile of Lupset. While the beseigers were at prayer one day in April, the castle garrison attacked them killing 42 men, taking more than 50 prisoners and capturing many weapons. Sir John was so dejected by this reverse that he lifted the siege and joined the main Parliamentary force in Yorkshire then engaged in the siege of Pontefract castle. In the first week of May a foraging party from Sandal Castle was surprised by a Parliamentary force which beat them back into the castle; the Royalists lost eight men killed with several others wounded and taken prisoner. Apart from the skeleton assumed to be Major Ward, there are eight further male burials within the castle bailey and it is certainly tempting to identify the eight recorded casualities with these eight burials. However skilled detective work by the paleopathologist Dr. Keith Manchester suggests that this neat equation may not be the true answer. No skeleton showed evidence of musket-shot wounds and only one showed evidence of a serious fracture. Two individuals died at between 16 and 18 years of age while the remainder were between 20 and 40+ years. In three graves small pieces of metal were found on the floor of the graves, probably derived from a mortar shell explosion within the castle during the siege. This could have caused death from soft-tissue injury such as to liver, kidney or spleen, or could have caused death from wound sepsis. However one of the garrison with mortar shrapnel in his grave was likely to be a non-combatant such as a blacksmith since he was powerfully built but suffered from a degenerative joint disease which would have made walking difficult. He also had a fractured fore-arm, an injury suffered several weeks before his death, perhaps when kicked by a horse he was shoeing; he had also suffered a recent skull injury caused by a cutting blow to the head as if by a swordsman. Another man had been crippled by osteo-arthritis of the spine. Dr. Manchester concludes by commenting that "although violent death with or without skeletal damage is probable in many cases, it is possible that death from disease has occurred leaving no skeletal evidence".

After the death of eight men and the loss of others through their capture, the Royalist captain John Benson left Pontefract Castle secretly with three men and came to strengthen the Sandal garrison. Towards the end of June Sandal was besieged by a troop of three hundred dragoons under the command of Colonel Morgan. Dragoons are mounted infantry armed with matchlock muskets.

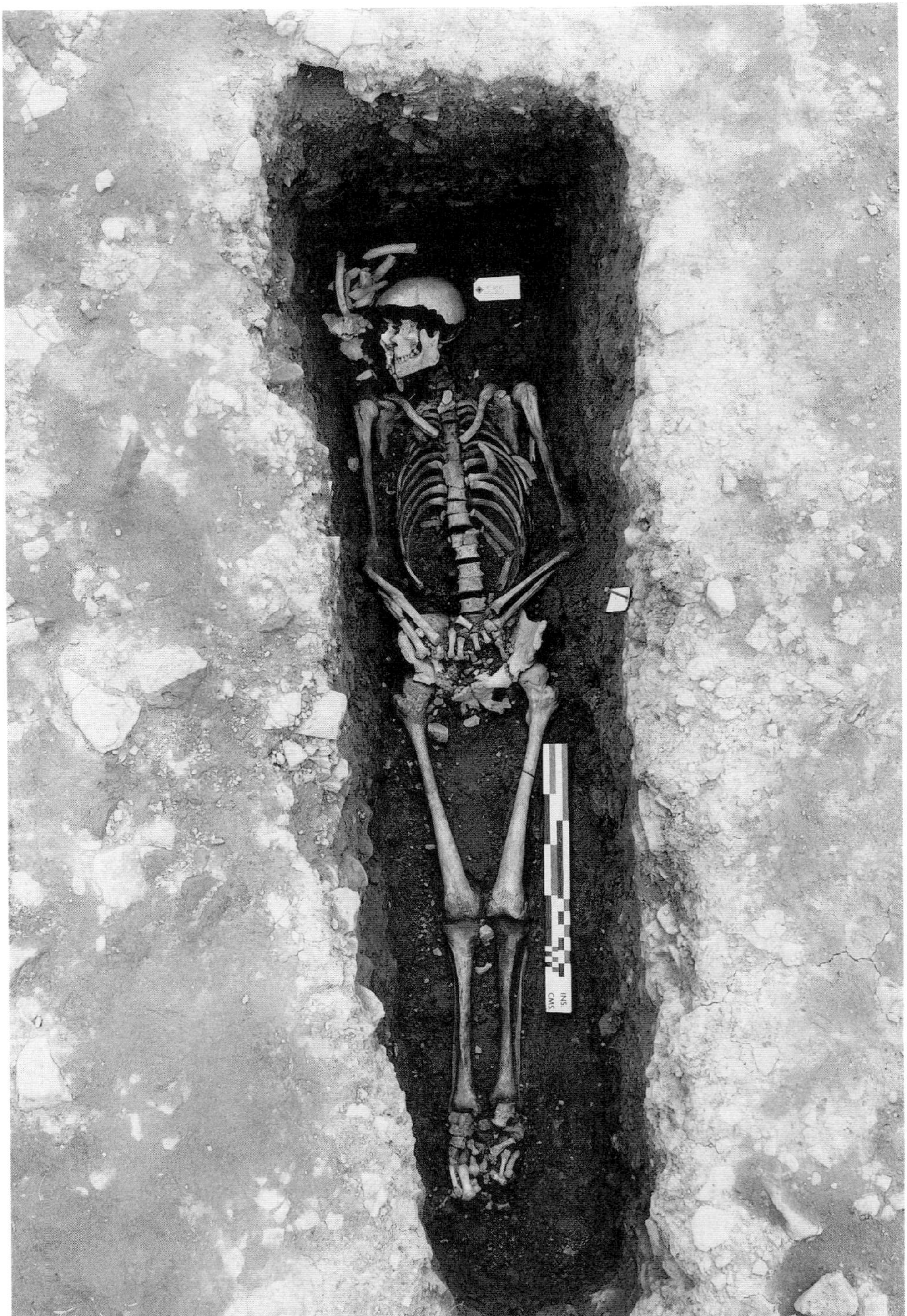

39. A Civil War grave in the courtyard

Lacking sufficient fodder for their horses they could not continue the siege and instead they withdrew to Pontefract though not without inflicting some losses upon the Sandal garrison.

The final siege

Shortly afterwards a fresh force under General Poyntz took up the siege and, heartened by the surrender of Pontefract castle after its seven month long siege, called upon the garrison to surrender. On 22nd July the defenders rejected this call but hopes of immediate relief were remote. Early in September Poyntz tightened the siege lines, obtained four "great guns" from Hull, protected them behind earthwork batteries and commenced the systematic bombardment of the castle. At this time Sandal was well provisioned and was garrisoned by a force of about a hundred officers and men. After several days of cannon fire some breaches had been made in the walls. Although the defenders filled the breaches with sods and loose earth it was a difficult task to stop all the gaps. On September 30th Colonel Robert Overton made preparations to storm the castle but after a parley the defenders agreed to leave on favourable terms. Having been assured that they would receive a safe passage to Welbeck House in north Nottinghamshire they surrendered the castle at 10 o'clock on October 1st 1645. The garrison was then 10 officers and 90 men with two of the men called "seniors" implying that they were professional soldiers rather than just non-commissioned officers. They also surrendered 100 muskets, 50 pikes, 20 halberds, 150 swords and two barrels of gunpowder: no pieces of artillery are mentioned. As a result of this capitulation only Bolton castle in Wensleydale and Skipton castle remained in Royalist hands within Yorkshire, but Sandal was "the most resolute of all the three northern garrisons" and its fall caused great rejoicing among the Parliamentary forces.

The bare record of the propaganda sheets issued by both sides in the Civil War can be given considerable additional detail by the archaeological evidence. The information gained from the burials has already been mentioned, but there are clear indications of which buildings were still in use and for what purposes. There is extensive information upon the personal weapons and the heavy artillery; there is the record of the pottery and the vessel glass used in the castle and the food remains represented by the animal bone and the shellfish.

The castle's appearance

The Tudor and Stuart building surveys give the impression of a castle falling into decay with cracks in the wall faces, shrinkage in the lead roofs causing water penetration and rotten timberwork, and some roofs with the lead removed by unscrupulous constables or their agents. Some upper floors lacked floor boards. It was this decaying structure that the Royalists attempted to put into a state of readiness (**40**). There is no evidence of how they used the main suite of state rooms in the castle bailey nor was there any archaeological evidence from the much denuded barbican tower. Probably the material from these areas and from the constable's lodging was removed when the site was robbed after the Civil War had ended.

However it is clear that the keep was used as a strongpoint in the siege. There was evidence of occupation in Richard III's Well Tower and in the room

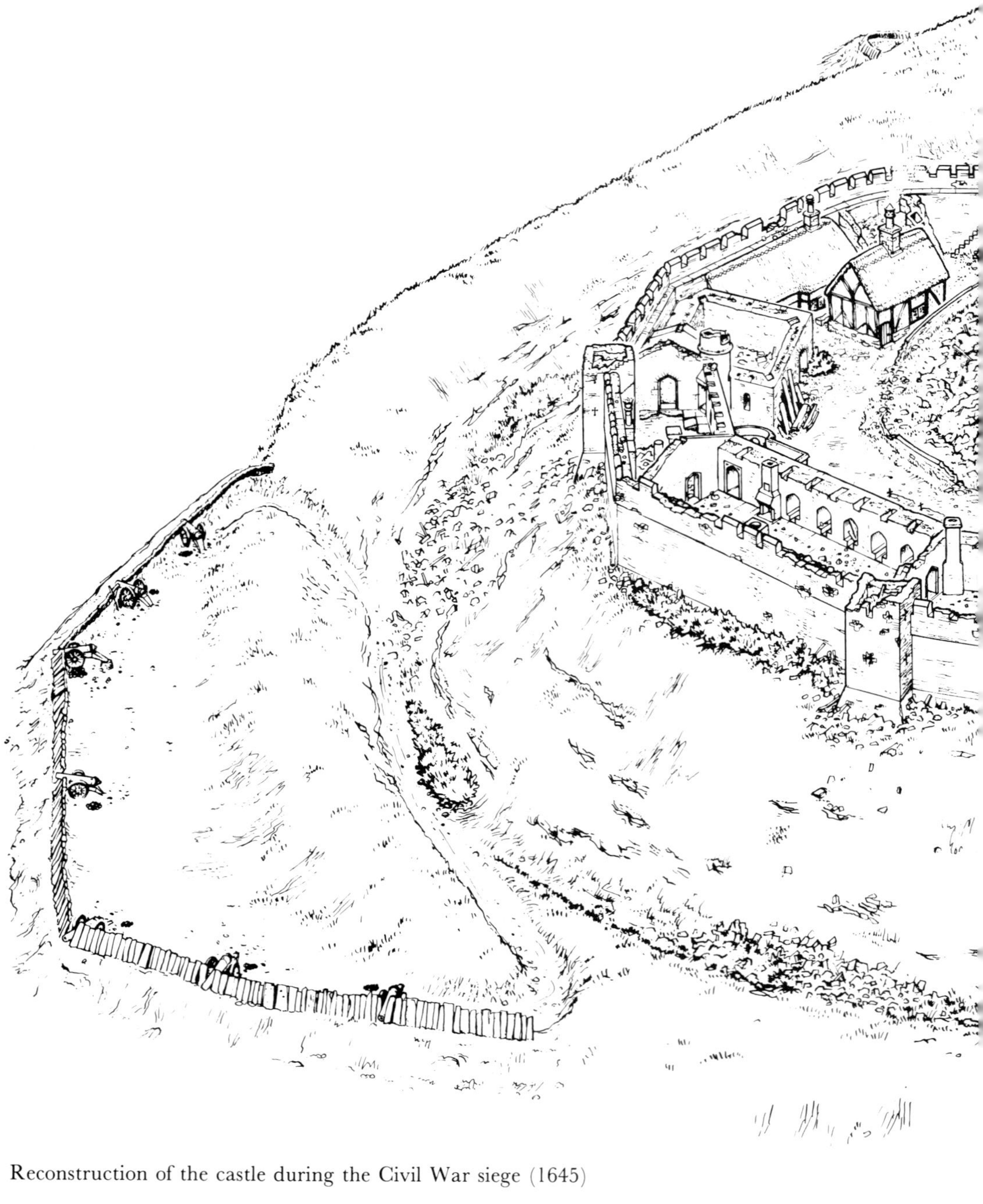

40. Reconstruction of the castle during the Civil War siege (1645)

just south of it. The polygonal tower bore the brunt of the bombardment. More than 40 cannon balls were found on the motte slope just outside this tower. The masonry is still pitted and cracked from the impact of the cannon balls (**41**). The well within the tower was filled with building debris, some of it accidentally thrown in as the upper storeys were made dangerous by the shelling but most of it the result of Parliamentary slighting to prevent the castle from ever being fortified again. Another indication of how dangerous the north-eastern side of the keep had become is revealed by the curving slit trench which enabled defenders to move from the keep entrance to the Well Tower in safety. This trench implies that the whole of the north-eastern sector had lost its external wall or was in process of losing it in the bombardment. The filling of this trench also contained cannon balls, lead shot and items of military equipment as well as the collapsed masonry blocks of a demolished temporary parapet; all this evidence implies that it was no longer in use as a safe passageway but had become a defended walk along which musketeers were positioned in order to shoot with a clear field of fire at the enemy beyond the castle ditch.

In the Tudor period the ditch around the barbican had been allowed to fill up with household refuse and the defence line was little more than a gentle depression instead of a steep-sided rock-faced ditch. This enabled the bailey area to be used more spaciously and the fullest evidence of Civil War occupation comes from the bakehouse (**42**). The new bakehouse and brewhouse were constructed for Richard III and may well have been as hastily erected as the "New Tower" on the keep had been. In any event the bakehouse was now in

41. The Well Tower, showing impact mark of cannon ball

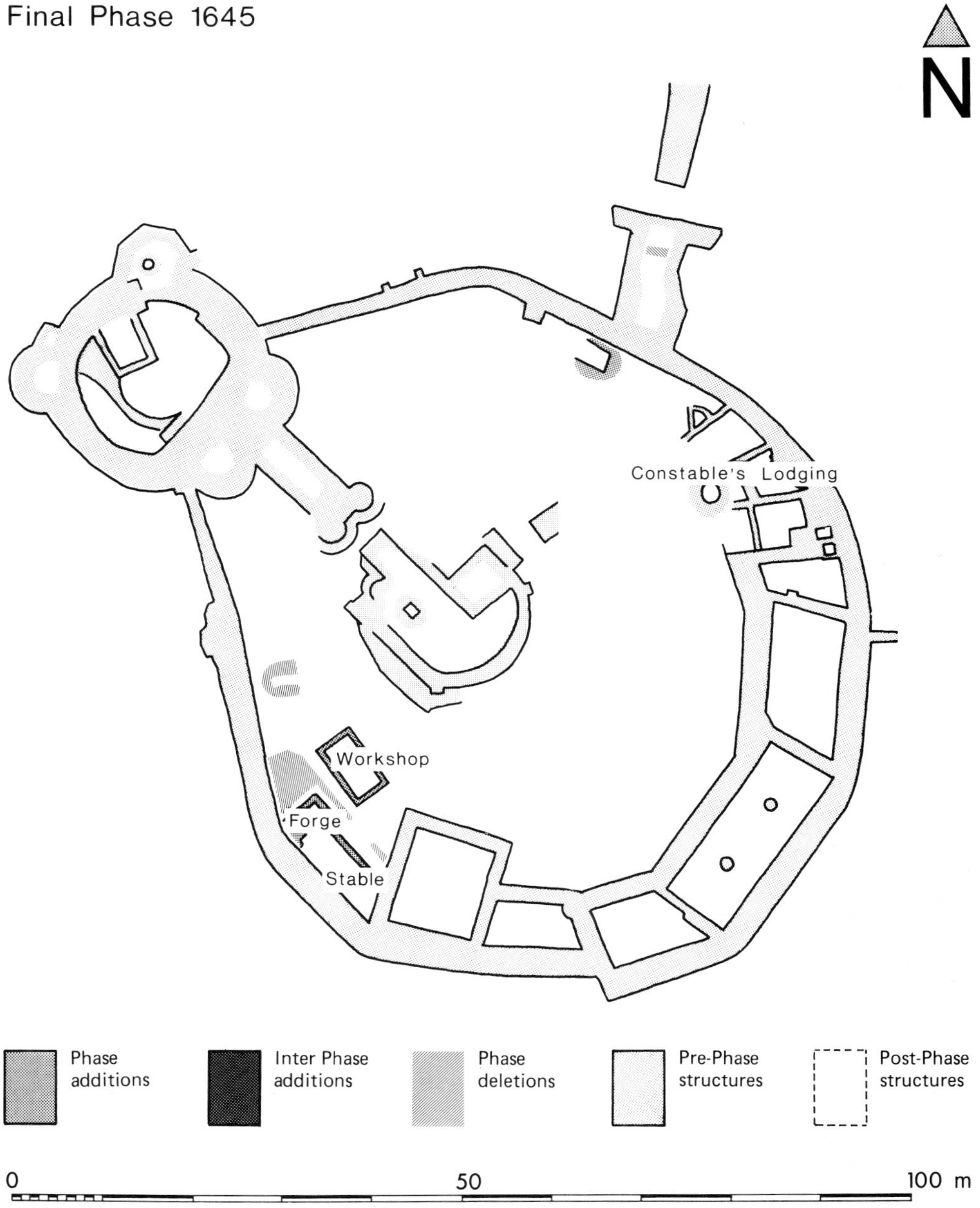

42. Plan of the castle at the Civil War period

disrepair and was replaced by a forge and stable set within the original structure but placed at a height of one foot above on rubbish accumulated upon the earlier floor. Both the rooms had thin walls, suggesting timber-built lean-to sheds set against the curtain wall. The beaten-earth floor extended throughout the buildings with a heavily burnt deposit of ash. The smithing-hearth and the quenching-tank were tentatively identified within the forge. Almost on the edge of the bailey platform close to the slope of the barbican ditch was a lightly-built workshop, a rectangular shed with quite insubstantial sill walls, presumably supporting a timber superstructure. The doorway faced the forge to which it served as an annexe and in the centre was a heavily burnt area. This workshop may well have been used for the repair of weapons damaged in the forays and fighting.

Adjoining the stable along the curtain wall was the kitchen with its frequently repaired floor and then one reached the two-storeyed larder with an awkwardly placed garderobe whose shoot came down against the kitchen wall and alongside the stair base. This shaft might be a lift or food hoist in the larder stores rather than an unhygenically sited lavatory. There were no other structural changes to the major buildings around the bailey courtyard. However in the bailey in front of the Great Hall were nine graves of Civil War victims, presumably buried in circumstances when it was impossible to reach the churchyard at Sandal. May be the Great Hall with its stained glass windows was used as a temporary chapel since that on the upper floor of the keep was unsafe to worship within.

Weapons of war

The evidence from the recent excavations casts considerable light on the circumstances of the siege and upon the diet and dress of the defenders. The attacking force of Parliamentary soldiers possessed superior artillery. Until Pontefract castle fell early in September 1645 the siege was likely to have been a desultory affair intended to contain the Royalists and so limit their potential for conducting damaging forays. With Pontefract under his control General Poyntz could pay serious attention to reducing the tiresome Royalists at Sandal to a state of surrender. The cannon balls or round shot show that the besiegers were already using demi-cannon (or "cannon of six": that is of six-inch diameter bore) firing shot weighing 28lbs and "cannon of seven" with shot weighing 32lbs as the main means of bombardment while the smaller culverin with its faster rate of fire using 16lb shot could be employed to cut out damaged sections of masonry. The siege altered in its severity when four large battery guns were brought from Hull, a Parliamentary stronghold. These were "cannon royal" capable of firing 60 pound shot from gun barrels with an eight-inch diameter bore.

Although most of the shot was found in the keep or adjacent to the Well Tower upon it (**41**), other cannon balls were discovered in the barbican ditch, in the courtyard near the gatehouse and in the outer moat adjacent to the gatehouse bridge. Arthur Credland suggests that there was an initial bombardment of the gatehouse before the main attack was concentrated upon the keep. The distribution of spent musket balls follows much the same pattern as the shot, suggesting that the Parliamentary forces entered the bailey having stormed the gatehouse and were therefore able to attack the barbican from within the curtain wall. Another powerful weapon in the Parliamentary arsenal was a mortar capable of throwing eleven-inch diameter shells over the curtain wall to explode within the bailey. Three of the buried soldiers seemed to have suffered wounds caused by the shrapnel of mortar explosions.

The excavators also found spherical stones which had been used as shot; these were to be propelled by gunpowder from small field guns known as periers.

It is likely that both sides used such periers, both from the discovery of stone balls within the bailey (perhaps launched from mortars with a high trajectory to throw them over the curtain wall rather than through a breach in the walls) and from the appearance of the outworks dug by the defenders (**43**). The south-east bastion was a hornwork of a type recommended in contemporary military text-books with a short length of rampart between two demi-bastions, joined to the medieval outer defences by earthwork banks. The sunken interior could be used for stores and for marshalling men and equipment, while the ramps could be used for dragging guns onto the platform (**44**). There is, however, no firm evidence that the Royalists had any field guns at Sandal; none are mentioned in the accounts of the fighting or in the deed of surrender. This bastion may have been dug in the hopes of obtaining some guns from the king's army or in the expectation of capturing some of the artillery being used by the Parliamentary besiegers. Three other small batteries were observed, dug into the outer defences, but these may have been occupied occasionally by Royalist musketeers as pickets or "forlorn hopes" to bring confusion among their enemies and to prevent them from

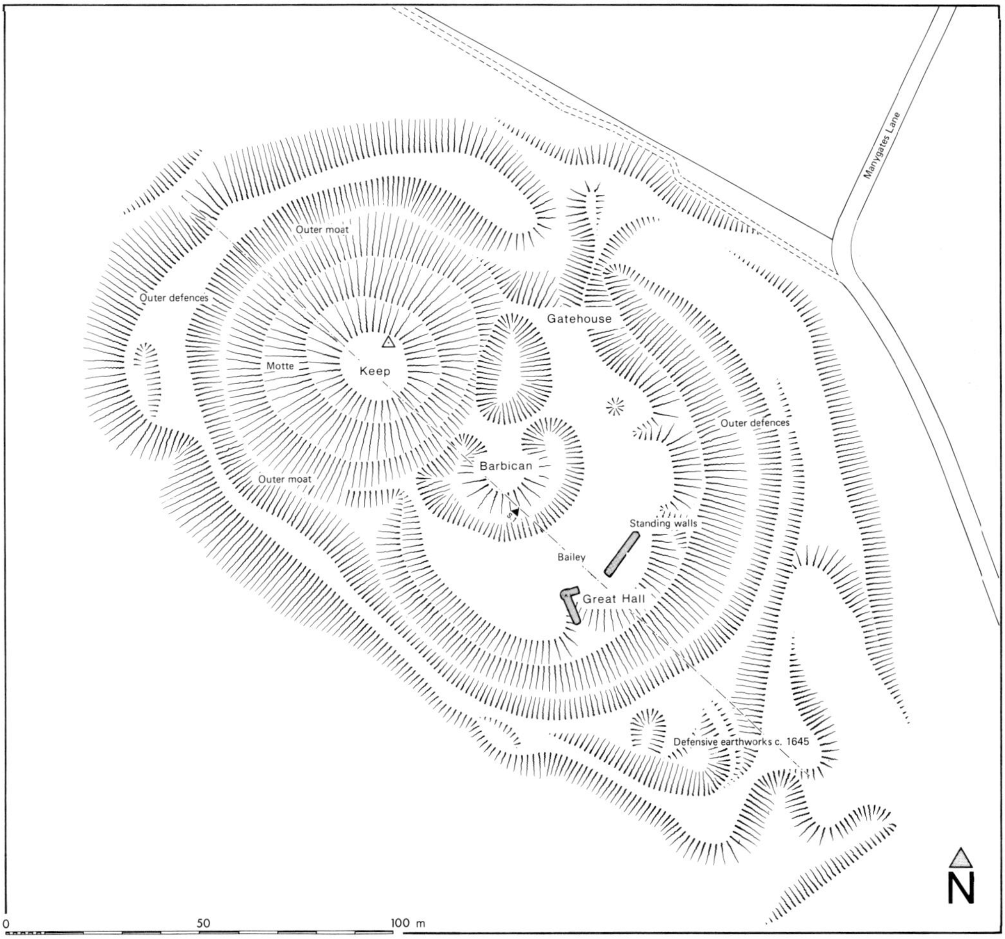

43. General plan of castle, showing Civil War earthwork defences

44. Constructing an artillery bastion: a contemporary drawing from Henrik Rusc, *The Strengthening of Strongholds* (1654)

approaching too closely with their heavy cannon. If that was the intention it proved to be unsuccessful.

One would expect the Parliamentary forces to have thrown up siege lines to contain the defenders within the castle. Certainly a trench to the south-east across the ridge leading to the Barnsley road would be most desirable; an earthwork battery to protect the four large "cannon royal" would be needed north-east of the castle when they brought their guns to within 500 yards of the Well Tower. No trace of any besieging earthwork has been traced on the ground, unlike the clear evidence of plough ridge and furrow in the playing field east of Manygates Lane opposite the school and near the railway bridge. In contrast to the sieges of Pontefract and Newark-on-Trent the encirclement of Sandal seems to have been less rigorous and to have lasted a shorter time. This may well account for the absence of visible surviving earthworks. Additionally the villagers of Sandal would have been anxious to restore their war-damaged fields to productive ploughland and safe grazing ground.

There was ample evidence for the equipment of the common soldier. Various metal parts of matchlock muskets, muzzles, triggers and priming pans had survived while the wooden handle or stock had rotted away (**45a,b**). The caps and nozzles of the powder holders worn on a crossbelt or bandolier had survived amid the rubble but the actual wooden containers for the powder had also perished (**47a,b**). A large quantity of lead musket shot was found either in

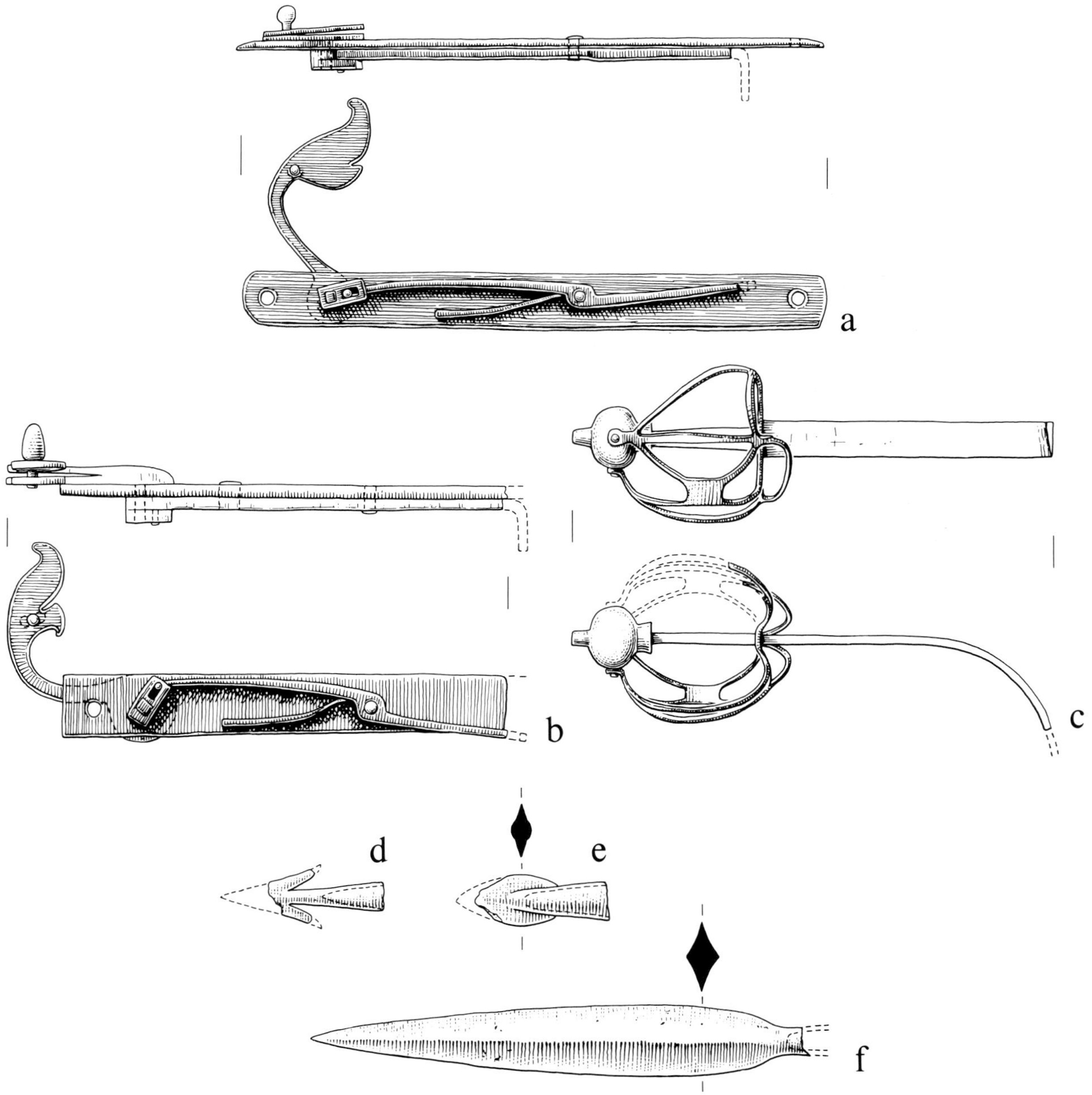

45. Civil War weapons: trigger locks from muskets, sword, arrow heads and lance

the trenches ready for use by the defenders or else flattened on impact against the castle walls when fired by the attackers. The foot soldiers were principally recruited as the musketeers; the cavalry would be equipped with fighting swords, of which six fragments were found including a fine basket-hilted hand-guard (**45c**). A spear head was also found among the Civil War debris (**45f**) as was part of a coat of metal plates, a form of protective body armour in common use around the middle of the sixteenth century and probably still perfectly serviceable nearly a hundred years later.

While the sword fragments showed the military equipment of the officers and cavalrymen (**46**), the horse harness and the spurs showed the everyday gear for horse and rider. Horseshoes, bridle bits, stirrups and curry combs were all the normal items of stabling equipment found in the Civil War layers, particularly in the forge where they would have been brought for repair. Nearly all the spurs

46. Civil War weapons: Royalist commanders, arms and armour from painted window glass at Farndon church, near Chester.

were plain functional types; only one highly decorated gilded and silvered spur suggested the Cavalier fashions of its gentry owner. During the seventeenth century the town of Ripon was the northern centre of the spur-making industry. However fifteen of the iron spurs were found on the floor of the forge, so it seems most probable that they were made or repaired at Sandal by a spurrier who had accompanied the Royalist garrison.

The need to pay the troops is shown by the discovery of seventeen coins of Charles I. There was a thick scatter of English issues on the stable floor, and Scottish issues were found in four locations: on the motte, in the north end of the bailey, at the gatehouse and at the outer drawbridge. All the coins but one were issued in or after 1635 showing that they were recent issues; the majority were of middle-range denominations, namely shilling, twenty-pence and half-crown. Three coins may be forgeries. While the group of nine coins on the stable floor may represent a single loss, the remainder of the Stuart coinage (and three coins of Elizabeth) probably indicate casual losses in the course of battle during the short-lived but hectic siege.

Food and drink

Another characteristic activity of soldiers is drinking and smoking. Drinking was a habit of soldiery developed over many centuries though the globular flasks from Martincamp between Dieppe and Beauvais in northern France suggest the more sophisticated tastes of the officers and gentry (**47c**). Smoking was a habit newly brought to England from the North American colonies, but the oval tobacco box of bronze and the clay tobacco pipes indicate that it was an activity practised by the Civil War garrison. The style of pipe bowls and the initials marked on the heel of the bowl show that pipes were bought from London, Hull and York. A few later pipes with the initials of John or Judith Gill may well have been made at Potovens just north of Wakefield and been lost when the castle was visited by stone robbers.

The pottery recovered during the excavations has a fascinating story to tell both about its manufacture and its use. The work of Peter Brears, now the Director of Leeds City Museum, has unravelled a detective trail worthy of Sherlock Holmes. As the castle had not been in regular occupation before the siege, a new stock of pottery had to be purchased to serve the garrison (**48**). It is likely that some form of bulk supply for the kitchen wares was organised rather than expecting each individual soldier to provide utensils for himself. Three families of potters in the hamlet of Potovens, three miles north-west of the castle, supplied most of the pottery found in the castle dating from the Civil War period. The kilns in Roger Lane provided 64 vessels, mainly blackware cups, costrels (drinking flasks) and chamber pots. The kiln which was possibly run by Robert Glover made most of the yellow-ware chamber pots together with some of the plates and ointment pots found at the castle. The kiln attributed to Jacob Willans made the large brown-glazed storage jars. Of the 209 ordinary vessels there is only one, a skillet or saucepan handle, which appears to be of non-local manufacture.

The relatively undisturbed state of the floors and courtyard surfaces within the castle means that it is possible to decide what was the total number and proportion of vessels used during the siege. The kilns at Potovens provided 87

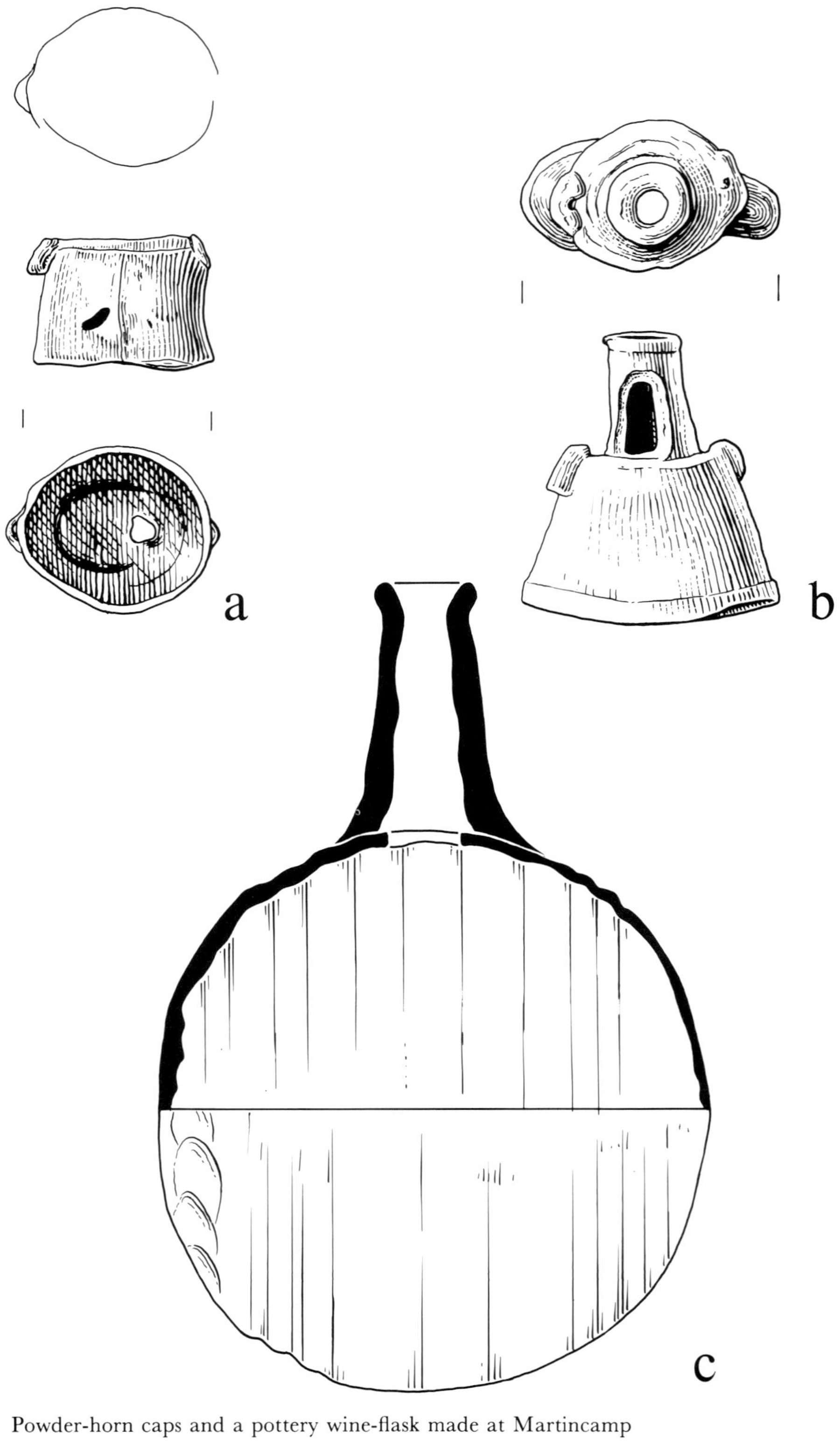

47. Powder-horn caps and a pottery wine-flask made at Martincamp

48. Typical group of Civil War pottery from Sandal

cups, 15 costrels (or beer flasks), 16 cooking vessels, 31 bowls, 19 storage jars, 3 skillets, 22 ointment or preserve jars and 16 chamber pots. Since the garrison in 1645 was 88 men and 12 gentry officers, it is reasonable to assume that each man had a pottery cup and that each officer would have had a drinking glass or a metal tankard. However the total number of costrels, cooking pots and chamber pots suggests that these vessels were ordered on the basis of one such pot to each group of 8 men and another pot to each pair of gentry.

This pattern of provision is also supported by the archaeological evidence about the circumstances in which the pottery was used (**49**). No longer was there a centralised kitchen and bakehouse, nor was there a communal meal served in the Great Hall. Instead the garrison was divided into a number of watches or companies, each catering for itself and patrolling its own stretch of the walls. Using the evidence of the distribution of the cooking vessels and related wares it is possible to identify each watch or platoon: one such unit was stationed in the Porter's Lodge by the gatehouse using the hearth there; a second unit used the fireplaces in the Constable's Lodging; a third unit (perhaps non-combatant) worked around the hearths in the kitchen and forge, while a fourth unit gathered at the fireplace in the centre of the keep. Further small groups of pottery in the Great Hall, in the larder and in the keep turrets probably identify where meals were taken whilst defending the walls; each group contains storage vessels for water, a number of cups and a costrel, a number of preserve pots, perhaps a bowl and invariably a chamber pot. The fate of one platoon sheltering in the centre of the keep is shown by the discovery of two tall cooking vessels, their bases against a small fire, and alongside them a number of animal bones. Apparently the defenders could not retrieve their meal as the bombardment of the keep brought masonry crashing down all around them. After this only the basements of the keep turrets were considered to be safe enough. The absence of pottery from the

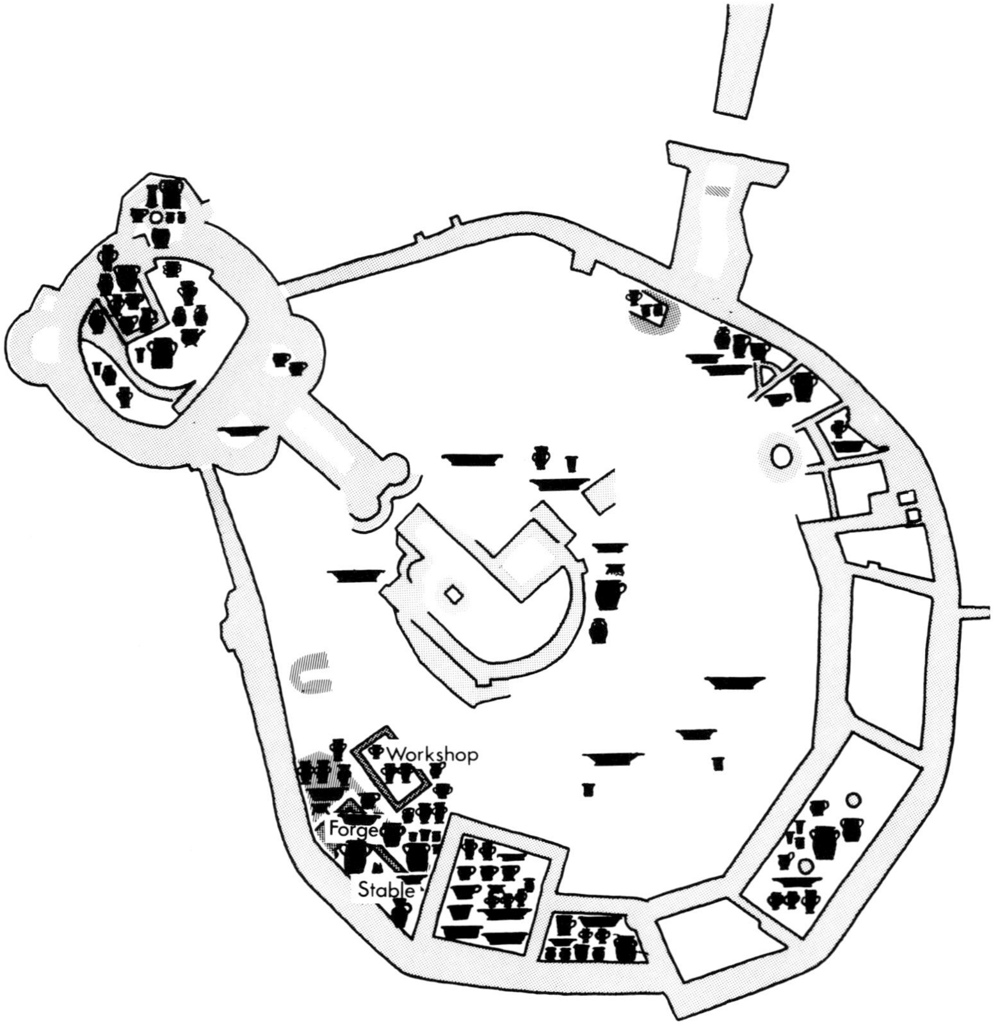

49. Distribution of Civil War pottery throughout the castle

barbican is to be explained by the subsequent erosion of the floor surfaces in that tower rather than in any deliberate neglect of the building during the siege period.

The evidence of the vessel glass provides insights into another aspect of the siege. Two goblets were found, both in crystal glass; one was in the keep, the other was in the bailey courtyard. The commonest vessel form was the bottle, usually cylindrical, occasionally square, a few were hexagonal. Four cylindrical bottles were found in the defenders' trench cut into the keep floor; perhaps they were needed there for medicines. Nearly all the glass found in the bailey area lay in or adjacent to the kitchen. This was one of the safest and strongest buildings in the entire castle with its thick walls, its stone roof-tiles and its absence of externally-facing windows. Its thickened fireplace and chimney would protect it from attack from the east, and the steep fall of the ground made it difficult to approach from

Milnthorpe on the west. In the kitchen there were found thirty glass bottles of various shapes and sizes and four pottery ointment pots of non-local manufacture. It is highly likely that this was the surgery or field hospital throughout the siege, particularly since the nine burials lay nearby outside the Great Hall.

It is possible to determine part of the garrison's diet by the survival of more than 6000 animal bones from the siege period (**24**: Phase +). The four main species represented were sheep (43%), catle (35%), deer, both fallow and red, (14%) and pig (8%). The special circumstances of the siege may account for the slaughter of cattle, sheep and pig as soon as they were fully grown; there was no need to keep cattle for milk production or sheep for their fleeces. The cattle were apparently killed as young male steers. Whether these were animals commandeered from the local villages or whether they were bought in Wakefield market is now impossible to tell. In earlier centuries such steers are not well represented among the animal bones at the castle so they were presumably not consumed at the castle or else were allowed to grow to full adulthood.

The horse is poorly represented in the animal bones. Presumably such horses as the garrison possessed were used for cavalry purposes and for transport. Until the final few weeks of the siege conditions were not so harsh that horse and other smaller animals had to be eaten. There were the bones of domestic cat and dog, of hare and rabbit together with their enemy the fox. Bones of chicken, goose and other fowl, together with fish such as the inland carp and the coastal cod, show how varied was the diet of the castle garrison in the Civil War occupation.

The pattern of the archaeological evidence confirms and extends the picture provided by the written records. We can see clearly the castle under attack, noting the impact of the cannon balls upon the castle walls, the casualties of war buried in the courtyard and the fragments of mortar shells showered down on the defenders. The castle was bombarded into submission and the garrison lived in cramped and uncomfortable conditions as they tried to hold out in the king's cause. When they marched away on the first day of October 1645 the castle had been battered beyond repair (**40**). The slow disintegration of its fabric was now hastened by wind and weather, by thornbush and stone-robber. For the next three centuries we must speak of a castle in ruins and not a roofed defensible castle any more.

The Castle in recent times

The end of the Civil War siege in October 1645 left the castle as a defenceless ruin. The orders of Parliament given in the following year were that the castle was to be made untenable. Presumably parts of the outer wall were thrown into the ditches. The gatehouse and the other towers were reduced in height. The result of the bombardment had made the keep buildings little more than a tumbled mass of masonry among which the defenders had formed gun platforms and access trenches.

Although Scarborough, which was supplied by sea, continued to hold out in the king's cause, the first civil war in Yorkshire was virtually at an end and Sandal castle had no further part to play in the hostilities. Its role as a prison and record office had already been taken over by buildings in the centre of Wakefield. The park around the castle could still operate when the castle no longer functioned as a country mansion. The castle's owners, the Nevile family of Chevet, made no use of "one demolished or ruinus Buildinge called Sandall Castle", nor did the subsequent owners the Pilkingtons who held it after 1753. Instead it became a subject of occasional antiquarian interest, of poetic and artistic inspiration and a place of relaxation for the steadily growing number of Wakefield's inhabitants. It twice attracted the attention of antiquarians: the earlier occasion was when it was drawn by Samuel Buck in 1719 or 1722 as the foreground ruins to a prospect of Wakefield from the south (**1**); this view was published in 1774. The second occasion was the publication of an engraving by George Vertue in 1753 showing the Elizabethan drawing among the Duchy of Lancaster surveys; other drawings from these surveys were published as *Vetusta Monumenta* (Ancient Monuments). The harsh shading of the engraving and the disproportionate size of the nearby trees have made this a less attractive depiction of the castle than that by Buck, but it has been reproduced many times in a multitude of formats. It is the only picture by which the castle can be recreated in its heyday even though the purpose of the original drawing was to show Elizabeth's Privy Council the cracks in the fabric and the faults needing repair.

As the city of Wakefield and the village of Sandal grew in size, suburban villas along Manygates Lane gradually encroached upon the castle fields and the ruins became treasured as an open space for recreation and picnics. It also became a place for celebration bonfires; a trigometrical survey point and much later a flagstaff were erected on the summit of the motte.

The first excavation (1893)

The Yorkshire Archaeological Society, then Huddersfield based, had visited the remains of the castle in 1869 but the first serious attempt at exploration was not until 1893 when a local historian, J. W. Walker, and a mining engineer, H. S. Childe, conducted a period of excavation (**50**). Workmen were engaged for three months to dig trenches to confirm the evidence of the Elizabethan drawing. In the more recent excavation these "Walker holes" were found as ragged-edged pits sunk to locate and follow wall faces. They seldom went to any depth so tended to record the latest phase in any complicated building changes. The selective nature of these holes is shown by the inaccuracy at some parts of their excavators' plan: the barbican tower is shown as fully round since only a small segment of the outer face was located. The "arcaded wall" was misidentified because the perspective of the Elizabethan drawing was not fully appreciated. The interior of the keep was not fully explored.

In discussing Walker's work it is often difficult to decide what he actually saw in the excavations, where he relied on the written Tudor surveys and when he based his observations on the Elizabethan drawing. At the gatehouse he can only have seen the outer part of that structure. On the adjacent curtain wall just to the south he shows a re-entrant angle based entirely on the Tudor drawing, unless he assumed that the outside faces of a garderobe were part of the curtain wall. The positioning of the outside stair to the Great Hall is inaccurate and Walker cannot have found the stair base or its column. In consequence throughout the entire domestic range on the south side of the bailey Walker misidentifies the buildings, naming the Great Hall as the Gallery and all the other buildings then follow in sequence. In the kitchen he certainly exposed the paved floor and the drain beneath it, but in the bakehouse he only saw the latest walls of the forge and the workshop and did not reach Richard III's work. Indeed where he cleared the reddened stonework at the back of the fireplace in the bakehouse, he equated this with the destruction of 1317. The curtain wall on the east of the keep is shown complete from the gatehouse to the keep: if this is correct then there has been considerable loss of masonry in the past eighty years.

This leads on to a consideration of Walker's faults in the historical narrative of the castle's development. There are three major errors. The first is to identify the earthworks as the defences of Anglo-Saxon settlers in the seventh and eighth centuries. In doing so Walker bolsters his argument by inaccurate place name evidence: Sandal was "the hall in the sandy place". Walker also relied on historians' views that such earthworks were Saxon forts or burghs. Prophetically in the same issue of the Yorkshire Archaeological Journal that contains this excavation report on Sandal, Mrs. Ella Armitage reviews General Pitt-Rivers' *Excavations in Cranborne Chase* and draws attention to the gap in knowledge over these earthwork castles. She emphasises that the only excavated castle, "Caesar's Camp" near Folkestone, was proved to be Norman and not Saxon at all. The second major error lies in attributing the stonework castle to John the seventh earl (1240–1304), mainly on the strength of his military reputation. In the absence of coin finds and with an inability to date pottery, Walker's dating had to be based on architectural evidence and he does note the occurrence of Decorated-style window tracery. The recent excavations have given greater precision upon this point. The third error lies in putting far too much emphasis on the private war between John the eighth earl and Thomas of Lancaster in 1317. Walker assumed that great damage was done to the castle by assault and by fire; he thought it was largely rebuilt after John regained the castle in 1328 with building

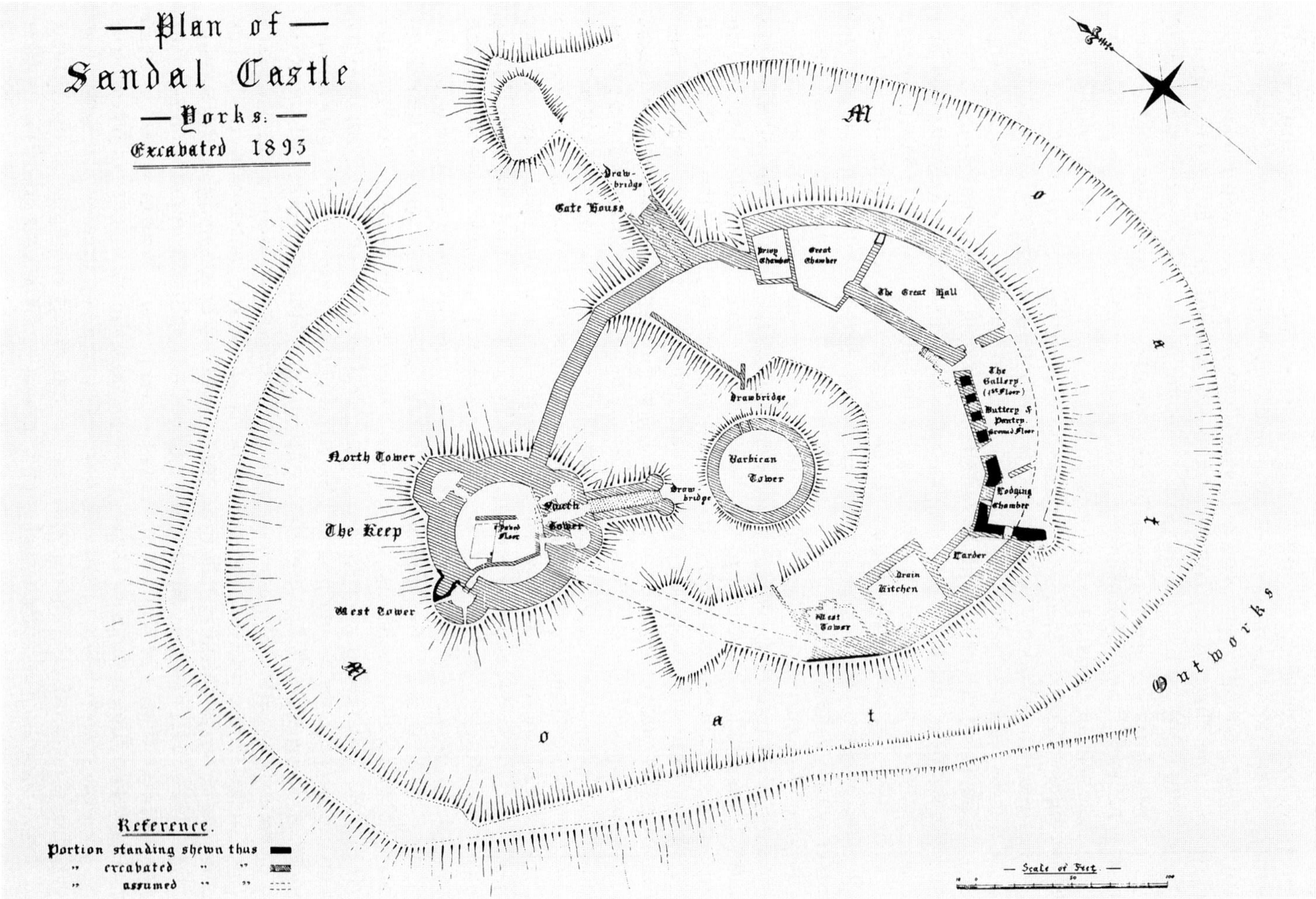

50. Dr. Walker's excavation plan of 1893

work continuing to the earl's death in 1347. Again the recent excavation has greatly modified this opinion and has stressed the role of Richard III as a builder at the castle. Walker knew of the 1484 documents but only identified the half-timbered Constable's Lodging as dating from this period. He failed to trace these lodgings on the ground, but in view of their flimsy foundations this failure is not at all surprising. The main criticism of Walker's methods is that he did not separate clearly his evidence of what he saw, what he assumed would be found and what he conjectured on the basis of documentary or pictorial evidence. He also did not separate the objective record of what he found from the subjective opinion of what date the structure was.

However Walker published his work promptly in 1895; he added many historical references and illustrated a medieval ring and a seal found in the locality. He continued to maintain an interest in the castle and in his fuller though discursive *History of Wakefield* (1934; 2nd edition 1939) he added a little more information. Dr. Walker was also a leading figure in restoring the monument to Richard Duke of York who died in the Battle of Wakefield; it stands beside the school in Manygates Lane, having been destroyed by the Parliamentary forces during the Civil War siege of Sandal.

The recent excavation (1964–1973)

In 1954 the site was purchased by Wakefield Corporation who had leased it from the Pilkingtons since 1912. With the formation of a Sandal Castle Joint Excavation Committee in 1964 a new phase of work began. This was a partnership between Wakefield Corporation through its Library, Art Gallery and Museum Committee, Wakefield Historical Society and the University of Leeds. The individuals most closely involved have been acknowledged and thanked in the detailed report. From Wakefield Corporation the drive of Councillor Deen and the support of the then Town Clerk Mr. Wylie were essential, from the Historical Society the influence of Captain Craven and the support of Mr. Ronald Fell, together with the hard work of Mr. Nock and Mr. Speak, was valuable for the project while from the University of Leeds the leadership of Mr. Philip Mayes ensured that the excavation blossomed in the early years while the author continued the momentum of the work and brought the publication to completion. What started as an exploratory work for adult education training gradually assumed the proportions of a complete and thorough excavation to the highest standards possible. At its height more than a hundred volunteer diggers were involved daily with a full range of supervisors and supporting staff giving their time freely and unstintingly. It is against this background that the success of the excavation has to be measured. It was not a government-funded rescue excavation but a voluntary effort arising from and dependent upon local enthusiasm and voluntary participation. Its most lasting result is the intangible influence upon a decade of Wakefield schoolchildren by giving them a good introduction to archaeology and practical local history; a secondary and unexpected result was that the supervisors provided the nucleus of talent for the West Yorkshire Archaeological Service.

The excavation started in the summer of 1964 on the west side of the bailey (**51**). At that time the whole of the castle was covered with rough grass, ragwort and thistle, dotted with thorn bushes and bramble clumps and shaded by

51. Excavations in progress within the bailey, 1966: looking west

a few larger trees rooted in the bailey bank (**4**). The motte slopes were used for tobogganing in the winter and for daredevil cycling in the summer with a switchback ride over the bumps and hollows of the barbican. Stagnant water stood in the outer moat which was fished for tadpoles and minnows. Apart from the two tall fragments of masonry in the Great Hall and the Great Chamber only a few stones poked through the grass where they had previously been exposed by Dr. Walker. Vandalism was a constant problem.

In the first four seasons of excavation the upper levels of the buildings in the bailey were examined; in 1968–70 the keep and barbican were thoroughly excavated; in 1971–3 the lower levels of the bailey, the inner moats around the keep and barbican and the eastern side of the castle were tackled. In the final year trenches were cut through the bailey bank and the outer moat in order to obtain information from vertical faces or sections. Also in the final year extensive work of landscaping and profiling the outermost banks was undertaken with the generous assistance of Wakefield City Council. Although mechanical help was used in the final year, nearly all the previous work had been conducted by hand and all occupation surfaces were examined by trowelling. It was this close attention to detail that made the often minor changes in surface colour and texture discernable. In parallel with this was a painstaking recording system for archaeological layers (**52**) and material finds which enabled the periods of the castle's occupation to be reconstructed so fully.

At the conclusion of each year's work a progress report was issued, often attractively printed and widely distributed. Additionally the results of that

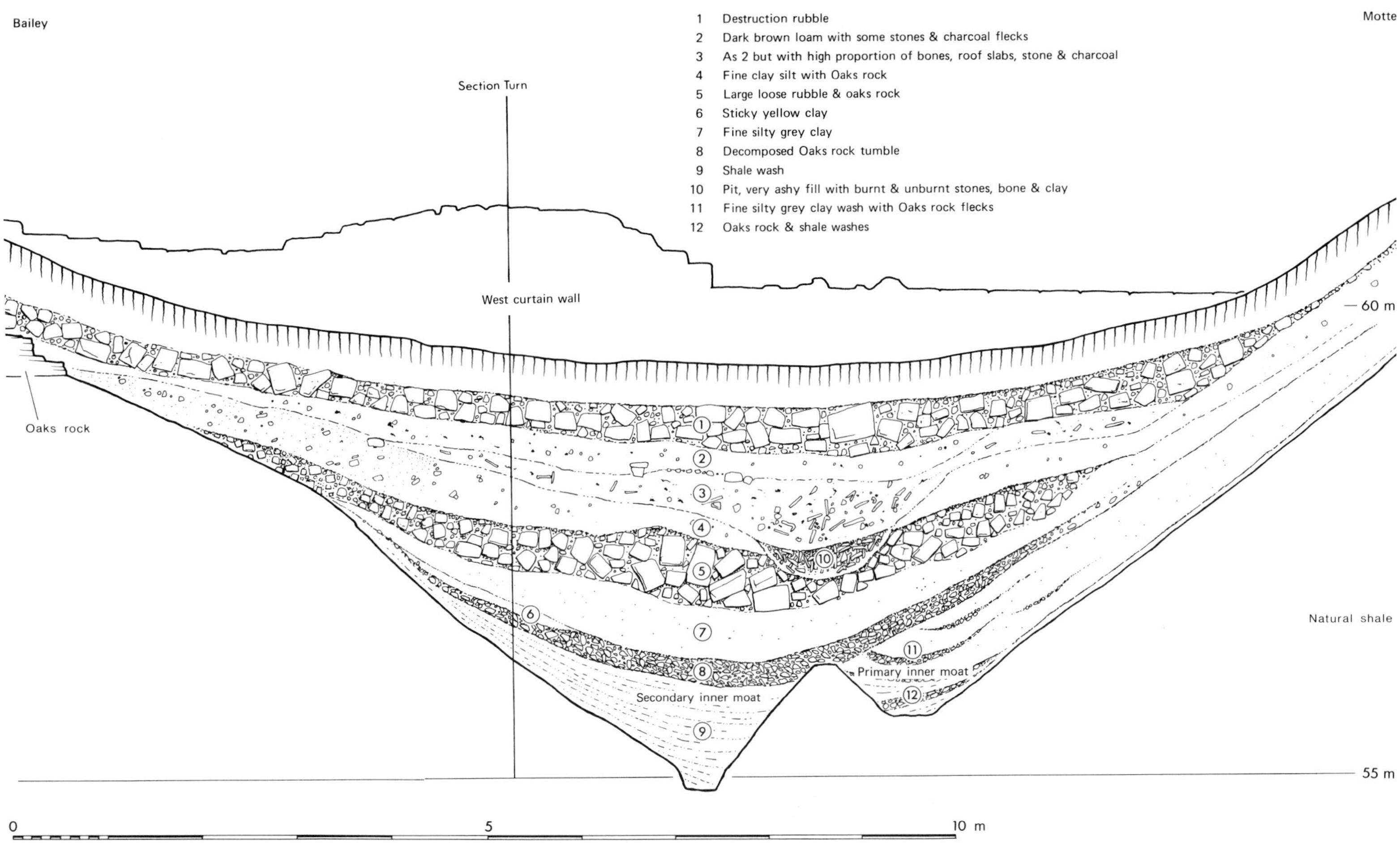

52. Section drawing of the Barbican ditch: looking west (S3 on illustration 18)

season's excavations were publicised in lectures, in training schools, in local and national journals and sometimes at international conferences. On one occasion in 1972 it was felt desirable to record on film a novel excavation technique using a "rolling section" creating a progressive series of vertical segments cut back at one metre intervals within the inner moat around the barbican tower (**53**).

There were many occasions during the summer excavation and in the winter's committee discussion when the final appearance of the ruin and its eventual care were discussed. It is difficult now to convey the sense of excitement as the castle stonework gradually emerged and took shape from beneath its cloak of obscuring vegetation. Particular highlights were when the pillar base of the outside stair leading up to the Great Hall emerged exactly as shown in the Elizabethan drawing or when the chamfered ledge on Richard III's Tower occurred precisely where illustrated (**33, 36**). There was a growing sense of understanding as the barbican tower emerged and equally one of disappoint-

53. Excavations in progress within the Barbican ditch, 1972: looking south-east

ment when the Constable's Lodging failed to materialise. The internal arrangements of the rooms on the keep were never fully solved: was it an open court or a fully roofed building? The burial ground for the Civil War casualties and the makeshift nature of the Royalist use of buildings was unexpected. All these various discoveries made it imperative that an answer should be found on how the ruin should be finally displayed. Invaluable help was given by the inspectors, architects and masons of the Department of the Environment's Ancient Monuments Branch (now known as English Heritage). Stonework was conserved at the highest level to which it had survived so that the final appearance of the ruin was as close as possible to what had been found in excavation. Some problems still remain which are mentioned in the concluding chapter.

The follow-up to the excavation was the treatment and study of the finds, the preparation of specialist reports, the completion of site drawings (**54**) and the editing of the detailed report. Much of the treatment and study of the pottery was undertaken in Wakefield while items needing scientific conservation were handled in the archaeology laboratories of the universities of Leeds and Bradford. Thirty specialists were involved in reporting on the varied range of finds from prehistoric flints to Stuart clay tobacco pipes and from seeds to animal bones. All the drawings were prepared in the drawing offices at Leeds University and the work of editing the final report and preparing a camera-ready copy was meticulously undertaken by Miss Shirley Johnson. All this post-excavation work behind the scenes had to be co-ordinated and timetabled; without full publication the bare record of excavation is worthless. It is to the credit of all those involved in the publication that they fulfilled the promises made when excavation started.

In the published reviews of Wakefield Historical Society's detailed excavation report the importance of Sandal as the only castle in western Europe to have been completely excavated to modern standards has been fully recognised. The thoroughness and the impressive scale of the excavations commanded widespread attention. It features in recent textbooks on medieval archaeology and four years ago was illustrated in the British Museum exhibition of "Archaeology in Britain since 1945". One aspect of the report has been singled out for especial praise: this is Stephen Moorhouse's pioneering approach to medieval pottery. He produced an analysis of more than 18,000 sherds from some 3,000 or more vessels to study fabric types and their dates, but more importantly he was able to study the way in which pottery was used and discarded within the castle, where it was used and for what purposes, whether it was discarded in one room immediately upon breakage or whether it was scattered in many parts of the castle. In this way a picture can be built up of pottery as an indication of social class; the intensity of occupation can be assessed and the ideas derived from the scanty documentary record can be tested. Pottery can also be used as a guide to trade; was the pottery obtained from local markets or was it brought in the baggage wagons of noble households moving from castle to castle around the country buying jugs in one nearby market but discarding it in a distant castle a hundred or more miles away? From his close attention to detail Moorhouse was able to suggest that a piece of Oxfordshire pottery probably reached Sandal from the south Midland holdings of Henry de la Walda, an early fourteenth-century steward of the manor of Wakefield, whose origins lay in the Buckinghamshire village of Wing. Similarly Grimston-type wares and West Sussex wares come respectively from the kilns

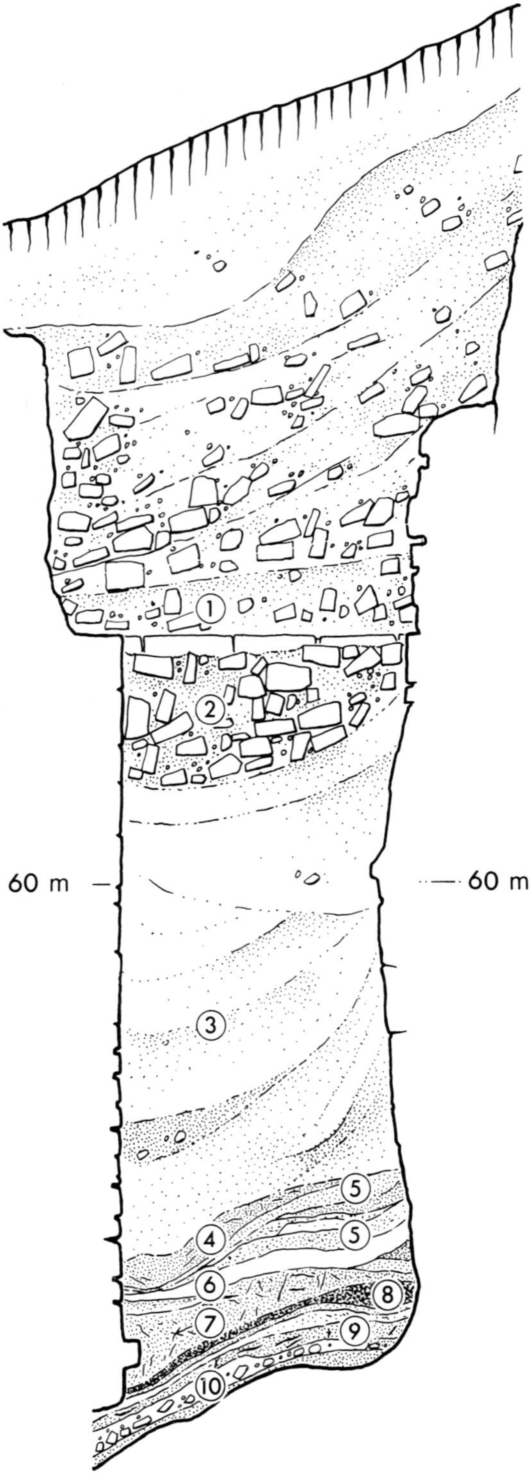

1 Destruction rubble
2 Heavy rubble
3 Garderobe infill of soil and rubble
4 Black ash and rotted vegetation
5 Sand
6 Purple silt and ash
7 Sand and black rotted vegetation
8 Black ash
9 Purple silt and black vegetation
10 Decomposed Oaks rock

54. Section drawing of the Barbican garderobe shaft

adjacent to the administrative centres of the earls of Surrey at Castle Acre in Norfolk and Lewes in Sussex.

Specialist reports may often provide tedious reading or be appreciated only by scientists in that particular field or a few closely related areas. There has been a tendency in recent years to place all specialist reports in less accessible but cheaply produced microfiche, though giving full coverage to the general conclusions based on those reports. This makes it difficult to check such reports or to compare one excavation with another. Far too much has to be taken on trust. The authors, editor and publication committee of Wakefield Historical Publications felt that it was much better to give all these reports in full, even if it meant that the final report was prepared in camera-ready copy rather than set up by a professional printer. The current debate on microfiche seems to justify the decision to make all aspects of the report and all specialists' contributions equally available.

There were times in the recent excavation when the next stage of the work was in doubt; there were times in the preparation of the final report when the magnitude of the task seemed to be beyond the available resources. However such has been the faith and determination of those most closely involved with Sandal that the work has been completed. With such a thorough excavation at Sandal it need not and indeed cannot be done again: by its very nature an excavation destroys the evidence in the ground. The past of the castle has been reconstructed from the stones and the soil, from the artefacts and the pollens. The future lies in the presentation and interpretation of the site to the public who own it and for whose benefit it is held in trust.

Postscript
The future of Sandal Castle

The medieval castle combined beauty and utility. Unlike abbeys and cathedrals which were built to the greater glory of God, the castle was built for the greater protection and promotion of man. If the castle possessed beauty in its clean masonry lines, in its decorative statues or in its dramatic setting, then that was entirely subordinate to the main purpose of defence, enabling it to be a safe haven for its baronial inhabitants and a strong rallying point for their tenantry. Its utility lay in its deep ditches, its high walls, its strong drawbridges and its commanding towers. Within these defences daily life might be cramped, smelly, tedious and short. The romantic glow which Victorian novelists and Hollywood film-makers cast over castles seldom existed, though acts of love, intrigue, heroism and devotion may have been played out within and around Sandal castle. How should, or indeed how can, this past be conveyed to the visitor?

There are three aspects to this task of historical re-creation. The first is the surviving structure of the castle on its hill-top; the second are the objects recovered by excavation which tell the story of its exciting past, and the third is the written record in whatever form it now exists.

In 1973 the last bulldozers trundled away from Sandal; the grounds were neatly landscaped (**55**). The masons dismantled their hut, leaving the stonework conserved. The main task of caring for the castle has rested with Wakefield District Council since 1974; they have admirably ensured that decay has been arrested and that the grounds have been mown regularly. The equally important role of maintaining and displaying the finds from the excavations and of providing an interpretative display has been ably fulfilled by Wakefield Museum.

The next step in making Sandal Castle excavations accessible to the public resulted in the publication in 1983 of the detailed archaeological report with its full account of the material evidence and the surviving documentary record. This detailed report has now nearly sold out and the time is most appropriate to publish this more general account of the castle, its history and its exploration.

These three interlinked aspects are firstly the concern for the castle ruins, secondly the display of the material evidence and thirdly the publication of its history. Taking these aspects in reverse order, it is most unlikely that further research will substantially change the main outlines of the historical narrative given in the preceding chapters of this book. The excavation report provides an unrepeatable detective account. This third aspect may be regarded as entirely satisfactory.

55. Sandal Castle from the air (1988)

In Wakefield Museum the objects from the excavation have been imaginatively displayed. By devoting an area to the Sandal material, together with photographs, documents and reconstruction models, the Council through its Leisure Services Committee has more than fulfilled its obligations to the castle and has succeeded in presenting it as a significant part of Wakefield's history. For the school children in the Wakefield area and for local inhabitants a visit to the museum will make a walk around Sandal castle an educationally more worthwhile experience. It is inevitable that museum displays are subject to changes in emphasis and to new methods of presentation, but in Wakefield there is sufficient material to alter and improve the displays when necessary.

However there is one place where a display is desirable when funding permits, and that is at the castle itself. The undoubted success of the exhibition staged during the summer of 1972 indicated the advantages of housing a display alongside the castle it sought to explain rather than at a museum two miles distant from it. Mounting a permanent display on the site during the summer months would be a highly desirable supplement to the fuller display in the city's museum. It would make the castle far more intelligible to the interested but non-expert visitor. With a good video commentary the castle would become far more immediately stimulating to school children keen to learn about their local history and about real battles at Sandal. The purchase of guides, post-cards and information about other sites and walks in the district would be far easier from a kiosk or interpretation centre on the site.

The major area of concern is the castle's continued maintenance and preservation. This is the most difficult problem to tackle because it needs an unpredictable budget and the District Council has a second major castle, that of Pontefract, in its care. The disadvantages of this are largely financial; the advantages are that the expertise gained at the one castle can be applied at the other. As at Pontefract care for the stonework and concern for the visitor's safety must be prime considerations. Conservation of the stonework exposed during the excavations was a priority in the period 1969–73 when the officers and masons of English Heritage (then the Department of the Environment) readily gave expert advice. Yet unfortunately stone conservation is not a single and finished operation; the stonework must be monitored to return to their original places all the stones dislodged by visitors' feet, by root and weather action, and more tiresomely, by thoughtless vandalism. Too many large stones have been tumbled into the ditch from Richard III's Tower. Some of the paved floor of the Lodging Chamber has found its way into suburban garden rockeries. Further regular maintenance will arrest this decay, enabling the dislodged stones to be stored until such time as their replacement can be undertaken.

Access to the site is excellent in some areas, particularly the bailey and the outer defences. The perimeter pathway provides an attractive and invigorating walk in most weathers. However at the moment it is difficult to reach the barbican tower without scrambling over stonework with the risk of dislodging the masonry or cracking the friable rock surfaces. It is impossible to climb to the summit of the keep without deepening the erosion gullies now disfiguring the motte slopes. These gullies, dusty in summer but perilously slippery in the winter, will eventually undermine more stonework and accelerate decay to which wind, frost and heavy rain will further contribute. It is the earnest hope of all who appreciate the castle ruin at Sandal that when finances or sponsorship permits there will be wooden bridges constructed where such bridges stood in medieval times. Then it will be possible to envisage how the various parts of the castle functioned for defence and for daily life. It will also be possible to climb up to the summit of the keep without fear of causing further damage.

To be able to admire the whole castle and the distant panorama of Wakefield and the Calder valley is to understand the impact of man upon the local landscape. This viewpoint where the flagstaff once stood is still a fond memory for the older generation of visitors to Sandal Castle. In its present state of ruin it is the complexity of the stonework and the massive character of the earthwork which continues to stir the imagination. Sandal castle still conveys most forcefully the part it played in the history of Wakefield and Yorkshire, and the role it occupied from century to century in the national history of England from the Norman Conquest to the Civil War.

CHRONOLOGICAL CHART

	THE CASTLE		THE OWNERS	MONARCHS	
1066			William de Warenne, first earl	William the Conqueror (Normans)	1066
1087–8		1088	William de Warenne, 2nd earl	William Rufus	1087
1100				Henry I	1100
c. 1120	First earthwork castle built (Site phase 7)	1106	William receives Manor of Wakefield		
c. 1130	Occupation of timber castle (Site phase 6)	1138	William de Warenne, 3rd earl	Stephen	1135
				Civil War with Matilda	
		1148	William of Blois, 4th earl	Henry II (Angevin or Plantagenet)	1154
		1159	William of Blois dies		
		1164	Hamelin de Plantagenet, 5th earl		
c. 1180	Probable start of stone castle building			Richard I	1189
		1202	William de Warenne, 6th earl	John	1199
c. 1210	First mention of a castle constable			Henry III	1216
1240	First mention of Sandal Castle	1240	John de Warenne, 7th earl		
c. 1240	Major construction of Stone castle (Site phase 5a)				
1270	Barbican under construction			Edward I	1272
c. 1270	Primary occupation of Stone castle (Site phase 5b)				
		1304	John de Warenne, 8th earl	Edward II	1307
1317	Local War with Thomas, earl of Lancaster (d. 1322)			Edward III	1327
1322	Sandal in royal hands & Survey made	1347	John, 8th earl dies; Sandal granted to king's 5th son, Edmund of Langley		
				Richard II	1377
		1385	Edmund created duke of York		
c. 1400	Occupation (site phase 4)	1402	Edward duke of York	Henry IV (Lancaster)	1399
		1415	Richard duke of York	Henry V	1410
				Henry VI	1422
c. 1450	Occupation (site phase 3)				
1460	Battle of Wakefield (Richard of York killed)	1460	Edward duke of York	Edward IV (York)	1461
1483	Richard III's rebuilding (site phase 2)	1483	Richard III	Richard III	1483
1485	Occupation of Constable's Lodgings (site phase 1)	1485	The Crown as Duke of York	Henry VII (Tudor)	1485
				Henry VIII	1509
1538	Building Survey made				
1545	Building Survey made			Edward VI	1547
				Mary	1553
1562–6	Building Surveys made	1566	Lease to Edward Carey	Elizabeth I	1558
1592	Further Enquiry made	1586	Lease to Sir John Savile		
				James I (Stuart)	1603
1610–11	Another Enquiry made	1619	Lease to Sir Thomas Savile		
				Charles I	1625
		1638	Francis Nevile buys Sandal Castle	Civil War declared	1642
1645	Civil War siege (site phase +)			Commonwealth period	1649
				Charles II: Monarchy restored	1660
		1753	passes to Pilkington family		
1893	Excavation by Dr. J.W. Walker				
		1912	Lease to Wakefield Corporation		
		1954	Purchase by City of Wakefield		
1964–73	Excavation by P. Mayes & L.A.S. Butler				

Suggestions for further reading

P. Mayes and L.A.S. Butler, *Sandal Castle Excavations 1964–1973* (Wakefield: Wakefield Historical Publications, 1983)

The detailed excavation report containing a wide range of specialist reports and a wealth of illustrations.

J.W. Walker, *Wakefield, its history and its people* (Wakefield: second edition 1939; reprinted 1970)

A general account of local history and the buildings of the neighbourhood in the first half of this century.

J.W. Walker, 'Sandal Castle', *Yorkshire Archaeological Journal*, 13 (1895), 154–88.

An account of the first excavations, together with a history of the castle and photographs of it in 1893.

Mary Ingham and Brenda Andrassy, *Sandal Magna: a Yorkshire parish and its people* (Bradford 1978)

Full of varied information, mostly about the last two centuries, and containing evocative old photographs of village life.

M.L. Faull and S. Moorhouse, *West Yorkshire: an Archaeological Survey to A.D. 1500.* 3 volumes (Wakefield: West Yorkshire County Council, 1981)

Volume 3 discusses The Medieval Rural Landscape including castles.

S. Moorhouse, 'Documentary Evidence for the landscape of the manor of Wakefield during the Middle Ages', *Landscape History*, I (1979), 44–58.

A valuable survey of the character of local settlement and the range of resources available to the medieval population.

General Reading

R.A. Brown, *Castles: a History and a Guide* (London: Blandford Press 1980)

C.P.S. Platt, *The Castle in England and Wales* (London: Secker & Warburg 1982)

J. Burke, *Life in the Castle in Medieval England* (London: Batsford 1978)

M.W. Thompson, *The End of the Castle in England and Wales* (Cambridge U.P. 1988)

R.A. Brown, *Castles from the Air* (Cambridge University Press 1989)

J.R. Kenyon, *Medieval Fortifications* (Leicester University Press 1990)

Glossary of Technical Terms

alembic	glass dome with long spout, the upper vessel of a chemical still.
bailey	an inner court or ward of a castle.
barbican	outer defence of a castle, usually beyond the main walls.
bascinet (*or* basnet)	bullet-shaped helmet, often with detachable face-guard.
bay	compartment of a wall or room between posts, columns or buttresses.
buttery	provision-store; place for issuing supplies or rations.
chamfer	surface made by cutting across a block of stone (or piece of wood) usually at an angle of 45° to the other two surfaces.
cistern	pottery container for storing or settling water, ale or other liquids.
constable	governor or warden of a castle, commander-in-chief of forces.
cucurbit	flask of glass or pottery, the lower vessel of a chemical still.
curfew	vessel for covering an open fire to prevent sparks escaping during night-time (literally *couvre-feu*: cover the fire)
curtain-wall	stretch of external wall, not normally supporting a roof, often between two towers.
dais	raised platform at one end of a hall for the lord's high table.
dragoon	mounted infantryman, often armed with musket or carbine.
fire-dog	metal support for a fire or grate.
fulling-mill	water-mill to drive mechanism for cleansing or thickening cloth.
garderobe	lavatory with a wooden or stone seat over a vertical shaft or 'shoot', often set in the thickness of castle walls, discharging into a stone-lined pit or into the castle ditch.
grave	1) place of burial; 2) local official responsible for a township or group of townships.
halberd	weapon combining a spear and a battle-axe.
hipped roof	roof with sloped instead of vertical (gable) ends.
latrine	*see* garderobe
louvre	opening, often with a turret or a lantern over, in a hall or kitchen roof; openings in the turret let the smoke escape from a central hearth and allow ventilation in.
maiolica	Italian earthenware of Renaissance period with coloured ornamental designs upon an opaque white enamel surface.
malthouse	room for preparing or storing barley in order to produce malt.
mantle	solid containing vessel placed around a glass distilling equipment to protect workers from the heat of a fire.
mantlet	protective shield, often used in medieval sieges; can refer also to protective walls placed as a screen beyond the main walls.
masons' lodge	temporary work shed where masons cut fine stone details.
mason's mark	a device carved on the stone by the mason who dressed it, to help the master mason's inspection for quality or for payment.

mortar	1) mixture of sand and lime to set hewn stone in a wall; 2) stone basin for pounding or mixing food ingredients; 3) type of iron cannon used for firing shells upwards to drop beyond the high walls of a castle, the shells usually burst on impact scattering lead shot.
motte	mound of earth supporting a stone or wooden castle tower; *ring-motte*: ring of earth bank supporting a wooden perimeter wall, often surrounding a wooden hall or tower.
oriel	large windowed gallery built out from an upper storey, either supported on a column from the ground or corbelled out from the wall.
paler	officer in charge of a hunting park, who ensures that its *pales* (boundary fences) are kept in good repair to prevent its animals from escaping.
palisade	fence of pales, vertical boards or circular stakes.
portcullis	strong heavy grating, which slides up and down in vertical grooves, being lowered on chains to block a castle entrance.
post-hole	a hole in which a vertical post has been set before it decayed: *post-pit*: a pit dug in order to erect a vertical post and then back-filled with earth and stones.
privy	1) private, as in Privy Chamber or Privy Council 2) latrine, lavatory or garderobe.
quern	hand-mill for grinding corn; the lower stone is fixed and the upper stone revolves.
ring-motte	*see* motte
sally-port	concealed opening in a castle wall, from which a sudden sally, sortie or unexpected counter-attack could be made.
section	vertical face of an excavation trench, usually drawn or photographed to record the sequence of soil layers.
sill-beam	horizontal timber at the base of a building into which vertical posts are set; may be placed on a low foundation wall or set or sunk directly into the earth surface.
steward	manager of a house or estate; the lord's civilian deputy.
stone-flags	flat slabs used in a pavement or path.
thack-stone	stone tiles used as a roof covering or 'thatch'.
thermo-luminescent	giving off measurable light when reheated; a scientific dating technique used for pottery, kilns and hearths.
truss	supporting framework of a roof, e.g. pair of rafters and a tie beam.
urinal	narrow-necked vessel of glass or pottery for collecting urine (for medical inspection or industrial uses).
visor	moveable part of a helmet, covering eyes, nose and mouth.

Index of Persons

Anjou, Margaret of, queen ... 51, 52
Aragon, Catherine of, queen ... 74
Armitage, Mrs. Ella ... 105
Arthur (Tudor), prince of Wales ... 72

Balme, Brian ... 73
Banke, Edmund ... 63
Bar, Joan of, countess ... 22, 24
Beaumont, Thomas ... 87
Beche, William de la ... 44–5
Bedford, John (Plantagenet), duke of ... 50
Beeston, Richard ... 63
Benson, John ... 87
Birkhead (or Burdett), Ralph ... 73
Blois, William of ... 19, 21
Bonivant, Colonel George ... 87
Brears, Mr. Peter ... 99
Buck, Samuel ... 2, 104
Burdhead, Robert ... 73
Butler, Dr. Lawrence ... 117
Butler, James, earl of Wiltshire ... 51

Cambridge: see Langley
Carey, Edward ... 73, 77
see Hunsdon
Catherine of Aragon, queen ... 74
Catherine of Valois, queen ... 50
Cave, Sir Ambrose ... 76, 77
Cavendish family ... 84
Charles I, king of England ... 72, 86, 99
Charles VI, king of France ... 50
Childe, Mr. H.S. ... 105
Clifford, John, Lord ... 51
Maud ... 50
family ... 84
Constance of Castile ... 49
Craven, Captain W.A. ... 107
Credland, Mr. Arthur ... 94
Cromwell, Oliver ... 86
Cumberland, earls of: see Clifford family

Deyvill: see Eyvill
Deen, Councillor J ... 107
Devonshire, earls of: see Cavendish family

Edmund (Plantagenet), earl of Rutland ... 51, 62
: see Langley
Edward the Confessor, king of England ... 6
Edward I, king ... 22, 35, 46–7
Edward II, king ... 24, 44
Edward III, king ... 24, 49, 50
Edward IV, king ... 51–4, 62, 64, 73, 79
Edward VI, king ... 75
Edward (Plantagenet), duke of York ... 49–50
Edwin, earl of Northumbria ... 7
Elizabeth, queen ... 72, 75, 77, 84, 99
Ellis, Mrs. Blanche ... 61
Eyvill, Thomas de ... 44, 45

Fairfax, Lord (Ferdinando) ... 86
Sir Thomas ... 87
Fell, Mr. Ronald ... 107

Gargrave, Sir Thomas ... 76–7
Gaunt, John of, duke of Lancaster ... 49, 50
Gaveston, Piers ... 24
Giffard, Walter, archbishop of York ... 22
Gill, John ... 99
Judith ... 99
Glover, Robert ... 99
Gundrada, countess ... 18

Hamelin: see Plantagenet
Henry I, king ... 1, 18–9
Henry II, king ... 1, 19, 21
Henry III, king ... 22, 35
Henry IV, king ... 49
Henry V, king ... 50
Henry VI, king ... 50, 52, 82
Henry VII, king ... 74
Henry VIII, king ... 72, 74, 75, 76
Henry (Stuart), prince of Wales ... 72
Holand, Isabel de ... 24
Hope-Taylor, Dr. Brian ... 19
Hunsdon, (William) Lord ... 77

Isabella of Castile ... 49
Isabella of France, queen ... 24

James I, king ... 77
John, king ... 21, 39
John (Plantagenet): see Bedford
Johnson, Miss Shirley ... 111
Jones, Professor Glanville R.J. ... 5

Kings of England: see Charles, Edward, Henry, James,
John, Richard, Stephen, William
Kings of France: see Charles, Louis, Philip
Kings of Scotland: see William

Lacy, Alice de ... 24
family ... 7
Henry de, earl of Lincoln ... 24
Lancaster, Henry (Plantagenet), earl of ... 24, 43
Thomas (Plantagenet), earl of ... 24–5, 43–4, 105
Langley, Edmund (Plantagenet), earl of Cambridge and duke of York ... 49, 54
Leland, John ... 75
Lincoln, earl of: see Lacy, Pole
Lionel (Plantagenet) ... 50
Louis VIII, king of France ... 22
Lusignan, Alice de ... 22
Llywelyn ab Iorwerth, prince of Wales ... 22

Manchester, Dr. Keith ... 87
Margaret of Anjou, queen ... 51, 52
Marshall, Matilda ... 22
William, earl of Pembroke ... 22
Mary, queen of England ... 75
Mary, queen of Scotland ... 76
Mather, Christopher ... 76–7
Mayes, Mr. Philip ... 107, 117
Milner, Brian ... 73
Montfort, Simon de, earl of Leicester ... 22
Montgomery, Roger de ... 10
Moorhouse, Mr. Stephen ... 47, 59, 111
Morcar, earl ... 7
Morgan, Colonel (Anthony) ... 87
Morice, John ... 73
Mortimer, Anne ... 50
Roger ... 24, 45
Moseley, Richard ... 45

Nerford, Maude de ... 22, 24
Nevile, Francis, of Chevet ... 104
Neville, Anne ... 62
Richard, earl of Warwick ... 64
Nock, Mr. B.P. ... 107

Overton, Colonel Robert ... 89

Peck, John ... 75
Pembroke, earl of: see Marshall
Philip II 'Augustus', king of France ... 21
Philip IV, king of France ... 35
Pilkington, family ... 104, 107
Pitt-Rivers, General (Augustus) ... 105
Plantagenet, Hamelin de ... 19, 21, 25, 27–8, 41
see also Bedford, Edmund, Edward, Lancaster, Langley, Lionel, Richard
Pole, John de la, earl of Lincoln ... 62, 63
Poyntz, General (Sydenham) ... 89, 94

Queens of England: see Catherine, Elizabeth, Isabella, Margaret, Mary
Queens of Scotland: see Mary

Richard I, king 21
Richard II, king 49, 54
Richard III, king 1, 52, 62–5, 69, 71, 72, 79, 89, 92, 105, 107
Richard (Plantagenet), 'of Conisbrough' 49
Richard (Plantagenet), duke of York 50–1, 54, 107
Robert, duke of Normandy 19
Roger: see Montgomery, Mortimer
Romilly, family 7
Rupert, prince 86

Savile, family of Lupset 73
family of Thornhill 73
Sir Henry, of Thornhill 75
Hugh, of Lupset 76
Sir John, of Howley 77
Sir John, of Lupset 87
Sir John, of Thornhill 52
Sir Thomas, of Thornhill 77
Shepherd, Matthew 73
Shrewsbury, earl of: see Talbot
Speak, Mr. Harold 107
Stephen, king 19
Strathearn, earl of: see Warenne, John, 8th earl
Surrey, earl of: see Warenne, William of Blois
Suthill, Henry de 44, 45

Talbot, Eleanor 54
John, earl of Shrewsbury 54
Tempest, family of Tong 73
Sir John 75–6
Sir Richard 75
Thomas, earl: see Lancaster
Tudor: see Arthur, Henry VII, Henry VIII, Edward VI, Elizabeth, Mary

Valois, Catherine of, queen 50
Vertue, George 104

Walda, Henry de la 47, 111
Walker, Dr. J.W. 43, 105–7, 108
Wallace, William 22
Ward, Major (?John) 87
Warenne, family 1, 18–21
Gundrada de 18
Isabel de 19, 21, 25
John de, 7th earl 21–2, 28, 35, 43, 105
John de, 8th earl 21, 22–4, 43, 49, 50, 105, 107
William de, 1st earl 18, 21
William de, 2nd earl 18–9, 20
William de, 3rd earl 19
William de, 6th earl 21, 28, 41–2
William (died 1286) 22
Warwick, earl of: see Neville

Willans, Jacob 99
William I, king 7, 18
William II, king 18
William of Blois, 4th earl of Surrey: see Blois
William the Lion, king of Scotland 21
Wiltshire, earl of: see Butler
Woderove (Woodruff), John 62–3
Wylie, Mr. A.I. 107

York, archbishop of: see Giffard
dukes of: see Edward, Langley, Richard

Index of Places

County names are given except for places in Yorkshire or for county towns. Countries are given for places in Europe.

Abinger castle, Surrey ... 8, 10
Agincourt, France, battle of ... 49
Aire, river ... 3
Aldborough castle ... 8
Alnwick castle, Northumberland ... 53
Anstey castle, Hertfordshire ... 51

Bardsey castle ... 8
Barlborough, Derbyshire ... 85
Barnard Castle, Durham ... 62
Barnet, Hertfordshire, battle of ... 52
Barnsley ... 20, 96
Bayeux, France ... 15
Bellencombre, France ... 19, 21
Belsay castle, Northumberland ... 53
Berwick-upon-Tweed ... 73, 74, 75, 77
Beverley ... 43
Bolsover castle, Derbyshire ... 84
Bolton castle ... 1, 89
Boroughbridge, battle of ... 24, 44
Bosworth, Leicestershire, battle of ... 64, 72
Bradford, university of ... 111
Bretton, West ... 5, 47
Brittany, France ... 7, 18
Bromfield, Clywd, lordship of ... 22, 24
Burgundy, France ... 52

Caen, France ... 25
Caerlaverock, Dumfries, castle ... 22
Caernarvon, Gwynedd, castle ... 38
Caistor, Lincolnshire ... 62
Calais, France ... 74
Calder, river ... 84
Calder valley ... 3, 11, 19, 20, 82
Cambridge: King's College chapel ... 53
Queens' College ... 79
Canford, Dorset ... 24
Carlisle, Cumbria ... 75
Castle Acre, Norfolk, castle ... 18, 22, 25–7, 40, 47, 113
priory ... 18, 22
Chevet ... 3, 5

Clitheroe, Lancs., castle ... 51, 77
Cologne, Germany ... 80
Colchester, Essex ... 86
Compostella, Spain, shrine of St. James ... 22, 60–1
Conisbrough castle ... 18, 19, 21, 22, 24, 27, 42, 49, 50, 51, 52, 76, 84
Conway, Gwynedd, castle ... 38
Cowick ... 47
Crigglestone ... 5, 6
Croydon, Surrey ... 22
Cumberworth ... 5

Darton ... 44
Denbigh, Clwyd, lordship of ... 24
Dewsbury ... 6
Dolforwyn, Powys, castle ... 45
Doncaster ... 40, 42
Durham, county ... 5

Eccleshill ... 6
Edgehill, Warwickshire, battle of ... 86
Elmet, kingdom of ... 5
Emley ... 47
Erringden ... 84

Falkirk, battle of ... 22
Farnham, Surrey ... 11, 68
Flamborough ... 3
Flanders, Belgium ... 7, 18, 22,
Flodden, Northumberland, battle of ... 74
Folkestone, Kent ... 105
Fotheringay, Northants., castle ... 49, 51, 76
church ... 62
Fountains, abbey ... 35, 57
Frechen, Germany ... 80

Germany ... 22, 57
Gloucester ... 86
Grantham, Lincs. ... 21, 49
Grimsby, Lincs. ... 84
Grimston, Norfolk ... 40, 47, 113

Halifax ... 57
Hastings, Sussex, castle ... 7, 8, 11
Hatfield, manor of ... 25
Haverah Park, castle ... 52
Heath ... 11, 84
Heaton ... 57
Hen Domen, Powys, castle ... 10, 15
Holt, Clwyd, castle ... 22
Huddersfield ... 104
Hull (Kingston-upon-Hull) ... 43, 75, 86, 89, 94, 99
Humber estuary ... 52, 57, 84

Ireland 50

Jervaulx abbey 35

Kingston-upon-Hull, see Hull
Kippax, castle hill 8
Kirby Muxloe, Leicestershire, castle 65
Kirkstall abbey 80
Knaresborough, castle 49, 51, 52, 57, 62, 76, 77

Lancaster, castle 65
duchy of 1, 77, 104
Langerwehe, Germany 47
Leeds, university of 1, 107, 111
West Yorkshire Archive Office 1
Yorkshire Archaeological Society 1, 104
Leicester 51
Lewes, Sussex, abbey 18, 19, 22
battle of 22
castle 18, 19, 25, 28, 47, 113
Llangollen, Clwyd 22
London 62, 74, 86, 99
London, British Museum 1, 111
Public Record Office 1, 76
Tower of 35
Louvre, Paris, France 35
Lowe Hill, Thornes 8, 19, 25
Ludford bridge, Shropshire, battle of 50

Maine, France 18
Malaga, Spain 80
Manygates Lane: see Wakefield
Marston Moor, battle of 86
Martincamp, France 80, 99
Meltham 3
Middleham castle 53, 62, 65
Milnthorpe, Sandal 46, 51, 84, 103
Mirfield, castle hill 8
Mortemer, France, castle 19, 21, 27
Mortimer's Cross, Shropshire, battle of 51

Naseby, Northants., battle of 86
New Park, see Wakefield
Newark-on-Trent, Notts. 86, 96
Norham, Northumberland 75
Normandy, France 18, 25
Normanton 5
Northampton 50
North Deighton, castle hill 8
Nostell, priory 22
Nottingham 64, 79

Old Park: see Wakefield
Ossett ... 84
Outwood: see Potovens

Paris: see Louvre
Peterborough ... 25
Picardy, France ... 18
Pickering, castle ... 7, 52
Pontefract, castle ... 7, 24, 44, 49, 51, 52, 62, 76, 77, 84, 87, 89, 94, 96, 116
honour of ... 7
New Hall ... 85
Portobello, Sandal ... 3, 51
Portugal ... 49
Potovens, Wakefield ... 20, 80, 99
Pugney's Beck, Wakefield ... 3

Raby, Durham ... 62
Raeren, Germany ... 80
Raglan, Gwent, castle ... 65
Rawmarsh ... 57
Reigate, Surrey, castle ... 18, 24, 25
priory ... 22
Rhineland, Germany ... 47, 80
Richmond ... 7
Ripon ... 99
Rochester, Kent, castle ... 22
Rougemont, castle hill ... 8

Saint Albans, Herts., battle of ... 50
Sandal, church ... 6, 73
see also Milnthorpe, Portobello
Saxton ... 51
Scarborough, castle ... 7, 24, 40, 52, 72, 104
Seamer ... 3
Skipton, castle ... 1, 7, 84, 89
honour of ... 62
Southover, Sussex ... 18
Sowerby (or Sowerbyshire) ... 5, 20, 45, 84
Spain ... 22, 57
Spurn Point ... 3
see also Humber estuary
Stamford, Lincs. ... 21, 49, 51
Stanley ... 84
Staxton ... 40
Stirling, battle of ... 22

Thornes, Wakefield, see Lowe Hill
Tickhill, castle ... 7, 52, 57, 62, 77
Tinchebrai, France, battle of ... 79
Tournai, Belgium ... 74
Towton, battle of ... 51
chapel of ... 51, 62

Ulverston, Cumbria ... 62
Upper Heaton ... 57

Valencia, Spain ... 57
Varenne, France ... 18

Wakefield, battle of ... 50–2
bridge ... 51, 62
City Council ... 1, 108
Corporation ... 1, 53, 107
Green ... 51
Historical Society ... 1, 19, 107, 111
Manor of ... 18, 19, 25, 57, 72
Metropolitan District Council ... 114, 116
Moot Hall ... 72, 77, 104
Museum ... 2, 114, 115
New Park ... 84
Old Park ... 84
see also Lowe Hill, Potovens, Pugney's Beck, Wrenthorpe
Walton ... 5, 11
Wark-on-Tweed, Northumberland ... 49, 75
Warwick ... 64
Wash, The ... 84
Welbeck, Notts. ... 89
West Bretton ... 5, 47
Wharfe, river ... 3
Windsor, Berks., castle ... 53, 79
Wing, Bucks. ... 47, 111
Woolley ... 11, 29
Wrenthorpe, Wakefield ... 20
see also Potovens
Wrexham, Clwyd ... 22

Yale, Clwyd, lordship of ... 22, 24
York ... 51, 52, 53, 57, 62, 99
castle ... 7, 52, 72
Grey Friars ... 72
King's Manor ... 72
Micklegate Bar ... 51
Vale of ... 43